LEARN GOOD CONSENT

On Healthy Relationships and Survivor Support

Edited by Cindy Crabb

Foreword by
Kiyomi Fujikawa and Jenna Peters-Golden

AK PRESS

Learning Good Consent: On Healthy Relationships and Survivor Support

© 2016 Cindy Crabb
This edition © 2016 AK Press (Chico, Oakland,
Edinburgh, Baltimore)

ISBN: 978-1-84935-246-8
E-ISBN: 978-1-84935-247-5
Library of Congress Control Number: 2015959296

AK Press   AK Press
370 Ryan Ave. #100   PO Box 12766
Chico, CA 95973   Edinburgh EH8 9YE
USA   Scotland
www.akpress.org   www.akuk.com
akpress@akpress.org   ak@akedin.demon.co.uk

The above addresses would be delighted to provide you with the
latest AK Press distribution catalog, which features books, pamphlets,
zines, and stylish apparel published and/or distributed by AK Press.
Alternatively, visit our websites for the complete catalog, latest news,
and secure ordering.

Cover illustration by Thomas Herpich
Printed in the USA

Contents

PART 1: UNTANGLING THE KNOTS

PART 2: HEALING AND TRANSFORMING OURSELVES

Acknowledgments and Thanks

This book took the work of many, many people—writers, activists, educators, readers, friends, and loved ones. It took the work of generations of activists, writers, and survivors before us, and the work will continue until all forms of domination and oppression are ended. Thank you for being part of this change. I personally would like to thank Caty C., Shari R., and Shannon O'Neill, for being there for me when I first began compiling these writings. Thanks so much to Suzy Subways for helping me re-envision the order of articles for this book.

Also, thanks goes out to publishers and magazines that supported these writings: AK Press, Cleis Press, South End Press, *Maximum Rock and Roll*, *Slug and Lettuce*, and all the zines and grassroots publications that paved the way and continue to provide a forum for brave voices.

Thanks to the organizations and collectives: Hysteria, Ubuntu, INCITE! Women of Color Against Violence, Creative Interventions, and all the ever changing community groups working to transform the world.

Thanks to all the people who contributed to the zines *Support* and *Learning Good Consent*, and to all the people who wrote and shared their stories in letters or in person. Thanks to all the people who wrote their own zines after reading these writings, and all the people who created and continue to create workshops based on these themes. Thanks to the people who have translated these writings in part or full into Spanish, French, German, and Hebrew.

And thank you for picking this up, for reading, for caring, for being brave. This book is for you. Thank you.

dorisdorisdoris.com

Foreword:
Water in the Tide

What *is* consent? What *does* healthy communication look like? How *do* we support our loved ones who have survived sexual or relationship violence? What can we do if it's *us* who have hurt someone? *Learning Good Consent: On Healthy Relationships and Survivor Support* promises no simple or formulaic solutions, yet offers places for us all to begin or continue conversations that are often silenced or shamed. It is a collection of powerful survivor's stories, conversations about informed and embodied consent, as well as practical skills and tools around active listening, setting and respecting boundaries, navigating triggers, and more.

These writings were originally released in 2005 and 2009 as two small D.I.Y. publications entitled *Support* and *Learning Good Consent*. It was a time when punk/diy/zinester/radical/queer communities, as well as some larger elements of the public, were realizing that "No Means No" was not enough, and that sexual assault was more often hidden within dates and relationships, hidden in manipulation or obliviousness. The idea that *consent* was important, that people needed to create full, non-coerced agreements about physical, emotional, and sexual acts, was revolutionary and controversial. Currently, this fundamental understanding that consent is essential is becoming more widely accepted, yet we need to broaden and deepen the public understanding of what consent, particularly consent that centers abuse survivors, actually looks like. *Learning Good Consent: On Healthy Relationships and Survivor Support* does just that. These writers recognize they don't have all the answers or solutions, but believe that it's our responsibility to learn from our mistakes, exploring and unlearning the hurtful dynamics that currently dictate how our relationships could or should look. The punk/diy/zinester/radical/queer communities that these writings came out of are just like most communities—we mistakenly believed that our "good" politics would protect us from violence; that sexual abuse somehow wouldn't happen to us, *or by us*. This collection of writing creates an accessible place for us to collectively break the silence and have a shared framework for strategies and tools that we can use and know that we are not alone.

How do we develop more concrete skills and practices for relationship models based on shared power, choice, and accountability? How do we respond when someone has been hurt, and we may be responsible? This book is both an important conversation-starter and resource for folks asking these types of questions.

The original zines came out when brave writers were self-publishing and distributing writings about surviving intimate violence and sexual assault, yet very little was written about consent. As radical communities, we lacked the tools we needed. Activist groups like INCITE! Women of Color against Violence, the Hysteria Collective, Consent Matters, Ubuntu, Philly's Pissed, and the Down There Collective were raising awareness. CONSENT IS SEXY was a common banner to see at events, patch to see on the back of someone's sweatshirt, sticker or poster to see distributed at punk shows. The writings compiled here were a part of the water in the tide of talking about assault, violence, and healing.

The impact that this collection of writings has had is wide reaching, and will continue to emerge and surprise us. These writings not only supported activists, queers, and punks in finding each other but because they were so widely read (at punk shows, conferences, theatre events, hot dance parties, book readings, and markets) they offered a shared foundation of language and concepts for many people in these communities to connect with. As the conversation around consent emerges from the underground into the general public, we hope to spread this foundation.

The questions in the beginning of this book about defining consent are a great handout for trainings and conferences; the Down There Collective's *Consent Workshop* inspired and informed many workshops and activities that were facilitated at music festivals, universities, conferences, and even at houses or churches for groups of people preparing to engage in political direct actions—any place where groups of queers, punks, and activists were going to be spending time together, you might find workshops/discussions centered around supporting survivors and consent practices. We are excited to see this spread.

While the content of *Learning Good Consent: On Healthy Relationships and Survivor Support* focuses very much on how we can individually express ourselves and engage in our healing and how we can support survivors in our lives and practice consent in our relationships, these concepts act as bridges for communities to place these skills into a broader and more politically focused movement. Principles and wisdom that support an understanding of the cycles of violence; a realization of how inadequate the resources available to both survivors of assault and also those who have caused harm are; about how calling the police doesn't always lead to an end to violence but can often further trauma for survivors and create waves of more violence for people who perpetrate harm and to their communities.

What makes any book, zine, song, or event powerful isn't just the thing itself, it's about the other things happening that are interconnected to it that creates huge momentum and gives power to ideas, demands, and hope! This collection is one important part of a wave that is still building up power. It's crucial while reading this text to also remember the other water in the tide.

In 2005, INCITE! Women of Color Against Violence hosted *Color of Violence 3: Stopping the War on Women of Color.* Over one thousand feminists of color converged in New Orleans to learn, collaborate, connect, and build power around the fight to stop state-based and interpersonal violence on women of color. Prophetically, this conference took place just six months before Hurricane Katrina hit, a disaster and lack of response by the U.S. government, which hurt, killed, and displaced thousands and thousands of Black New Orleans residents.

In 2006, Ubuntu—a woman of color and survivor-led collective—formed in Durham, North Carolina in response to the brutal rape of a Black woman by members of the Duke Lacrosse team. Ubuntu's work utilizes education, facilitated community dialogue, accountability processes, art, and tight political organizing. The collective's name, borrowed from the Sub-Saharan African concept, *Ubuntu*, translates roughly to *I am because we are.*

Just two years after the *Support* zine came out, Generation Five—an organization committed to ending childhood sexual abuse in the next five generations—published one of this movement's most influential resources. *Toward Transformative Justice*, a ninety-page document that articulates the ways in which "individual justice and collective liberation are equally important, mutually supportive, and fundamentally intertwined."

In 2009, Creative Interventions began one of its most inspiring projects, the Story Telling and Organizing Project (STOP), a community project that collects and shares the stories of "everyday people ending violence through collective, community-based alternatives." Creative Interventions is a community resource center committed to sharing tools to interrupt violence. Open to all, Creative Interventions aims to bolster the sustainability and healing of communities of color, queer, and immigrant communities.

There were, of course, many more powerful organizations and collectives as well as important moments in the anti-violence movement, but the above offer us insight into the landscape of the movements these writings were running parallel to.

What's in front of us now?

The conversations about consent that were happening both during the creation of—and also because of—these writings led communities to define consent even further, placing it within a framework of structural inequality and oppression (i.e. racism, sexism, classism, ableism, adultism, colonialism, heterosexism, cis-sexism, etc). We know that oppression limits our choices and limits our ability to have meaningful, decision-making power over parts of our lives. How then do we navigate the ways we have choice, agency, and consent in a way that also acknowledges the societal power that we are either privileged with or that comes at our expense?

Part of the framework of developing relationship skills around consent, listening, and accountability lends itself to a model that assumes rape, sexual abuse, and other forms of violence will be eliminated when we have the skills to name, hear, and respect our boundaries, desires, and needs. While this work is vital, it will not—on its own—radically alter the fundamental structural inequalities that are causing violence to happen. While these writings lay out the tools for us to begin addressing our interpersonal relationships, our movements ask us to keep going. The ideas in these writings offer us poetic and fierce language to name why shifting the imbalances of power, breaking silence, and fighting *and* loving for safe and liberatory relationships, is vital.

Some of our work moving forward is applying these individual tools to a collective responsibility. Expecting that we, as broad communities, must understand the ways that *structural inequities* generate violence, complicate our abilities to consent, and stand in the our way of our healing.

The ideas and concepts in this book are the roots we individually plant. Our commitment to fighting for a world with racial, economic, gender, and disability justice are the water, soil, and nutrients that feed our work.

We know we don't need to be healed to do this work. *Learning Good Consent* offers tools to stay in the movement and our communities—and shift the responses to violence that shame, blame, re-victimize, or deny survivors. They remind us that we can't always wait to heal from the hurt we've experienced before we are ready to be a part of our communities, to fight for social justice. Our healing is ongoing, it's powerful, and it's a valuable tool.

For these skills and tools to work, we must continually re-think and practice them, however we must also fight to change the large and violent systems that surround us and create the conditions in which we are trying to survive.

So the collection of writings you have in front of you is a primer for supporting yourself, your friends, and your loved ones. It's a toolkit you can use to help have the relationships and communication you want—ones based on respect, shared power, and choice. It's an attempt to untangle the tricky power dynamics we are all navigating. It's a permission slip to continue your healing, to connect, and to move up the ways you support survivors and work to end violence. It's an artifact from all the dialogues, skill-building sessions, and tides that were (and continue) rising to end sexual abuse in the 00s, specifically within diy/punk/zine/queer communities. It's a window of hope into a world without abuse. It's not a one-size-fits-all solution or all-knowing oracle that shows us how the world will be, but it's got an atlas with some ideas on how we might get there.

We hope it will also be a springboard to further engaging in broader movements—and the start of recognizing that we need more skills to move from our values, as well as a broader structure to support us in this work. We hope it will be an invitation to the simultaneous dialogues and movements that are happening amongst feminists of color—at fabulous organizations like INCITE!, Creative Interventions, Black Lives Matter, and Audre Lorde Project, to name just a few. Dialogues that remind us that our strategies to end violence cannot rely on systems that further perpetuate violence against communities of color, poor people, undocumented people, people with disabilities, queer and trans people, and many others.

We hope you enjoy *Learning Good Consent*. We can't wait to see how the energy, smarts, and brilliance of today's movements take these ideas to build up more powerful waves.

Kiyomi Fujikawa & Jenna Peters-Golden
of Philly Stands Up! Collective

PART 1

Untangling the Knots

Heads Up

Kiyomi Fujikawa, Jenna Peters-Golden
& Cindy Crabb

Hello! The following writings focus on topics of sexual abuse and violence. As these are often heavy and sometimes triggering topics, we encourage you to read with care and give yourself some extra support and tenderness. Consider taking a moment to take stock of the resources that you have. What do you do to take care of yourself when you are scared? Do you have people you can turn to or call? Activities that help ease the pain? Images that bring you peace?

Personal ways you practice grounding and resilience? Other tools and strategies that could help?

Please take care of yourself and reach out as you need to.

Pages 133 and 139 in this book offer some helpful tools for managing triggers and crisis.

Here are some helpful links and hotline numbers:

1. https://rainn.org/

2. http://farout.org/2013/10/21/mapping-our-collective-wellness/

3. 1-800-656-HOPE (4673) is the number of a crisis line or text "START" to 741-741 for free and confidential crisis support over text.

Can we talk about language for a second?

To prepare you to engage with the ideas, assessments, and practices in the rest of this book, some quick definitions might be in order. There is no single way to use language and none of this language is perfect or static, but these descriptions should help all readers be on the same page.

SURVIVOR: Someone who has experienced assault, violence, or co-ercion. This can be physical, sexual, or emotional in nature. We use the term "survivor" because it connotes agency and self-determination. Survivors are people who are still with us, victims are those who are not. We honor all the ways people survive violence—including when they fall outside an idealized stereotype of how a survivor is "supposed" to act. For more on this, check out Emi Koyama's brilliant work on *Negative Survivorship* at http://harmreduction.org/wp-content/uploads/2013/01/Negative_Survivorship_HRC_Public.pdf.

PERPETRATOR OR PERSON WHO CAUSED HARM: Since the original publication of these writings, much conversation has happened in anti-violence and activist communities. Many different terms identify someone who has assaulted or violated someone else: abuser, aggressor, perpetrator, violator. There has been a push from the Transformative Justice movements to use a term that identifies a person's action(s) instead of a term that defines them *by* their action(s), so now days we often use terms like "person who caused harm," or "person who perpetrated violence."

CONSENT: Full, non-coerced agreement between all parties about physical, emotional, and sexual acts and dynamics. Getting agreement needs to be explicit and must take verbal and body language into account.

BOUNDARY: A limit, line, or marker that designates both what someone may be okay with or not okay with. Some boundaries are flexible and fluid and can change, while other boundaries are hard and rigid. Part of consent is hearing and respecting people's boundaries.

TRIGGER: A trigger is when something you hear, see, feel, or experience somehow wakes up memories, senses, and parts of your body—it might transport you back to a time of experiencing trauma. Sometimes getting triggered can feel scary and negative. Sometimes it might be positive: it can bring you back to your body and an experience that perhaps you were dissociated from.

ACCOUNTABLE: Engaging in the work to address harm you've committed, participate in pathways for healing, and commit to changing your behavior in an effort to make sure you don't commit harm again. Being accountable might also ask someone to work with other people in a community to participate in bigger cultural and political transformations that are at the root of stopping violence.

ACCOUNTABILITY PROCESS: An organized and intentional effort for someone (or a group) to understand and change the behaviors that led to violence, crossing boundaries, or abuse. There are many different models of accountability processes, but they often involve friends or community members serving the role of support/facilitator.

Consent Questions

Cindy Crabb & Andrea Golden

The project of this book started with a list of questions. We wondered, if most assaults happened within relationships, dates, and amongst people who knew each other, why we always talk about assault as if it was something "bad" people did, not something we and our friends did. Almost everyone I knew had been in sexual situations that lacked consent with people in our own community. Andrea came to me with the proposal that we write up a list of questions and hold a community-wide discussion with the hopes that it would help people to think deeply, and to help open up conversations about consent. The feedback we got was incredible. People used these questions to talk to their partners, their friends, in groups, in couples, alone. People were able to name their desires, name their problematic behaviors, define their boundaries, and think clearly, some of them for the first time. People took the list and translated it, changed it, added to it, reprinted it, created workshops inspired by it. This list of questions has proven to be an amazing place to start talking about the complexities of consent.

We know it's a long list, but please read and think honestly about these questions, one at a time.

1. How do you define consent?

2. Have you ever talked about consent with your partners(s) or friends?

3. Do you know people, or have you been with people who define consent differently than you do?

4. Have you ever been unsure about whether or not the person you were being sexual with wanted to be doing what you were doing? Did you talk about it? Did you ignore it in hopes that it would change? Did you continue what you were doing because it was

pleasurable to you and you didn't want to deal with what the other person was experiencing? Did you continue because you felt it was your duty? How do you feel about the choice you made?

5. Do you think it is the other person's responsibility to say something if they aren't into what you are doing?

6. How might someone express that what is happening is not OK?

7. Do you look only for verbal signs or are there other signs?

8. Do you think it is possible to misinterpret silence for consent?

9. Have you ever asked someone what kinds of signs you should look for if they have a hard time verbalizing when something feels wrong?

10. Do you only ask about these kinds of things if you are in a serious relationship or do you feel able to talk in casual situations too?

11. Do you think talking ruins the mood?

12. Do you think consent can be erotic?

13. Do you think about people's abuse histories?

14. Do you check in as things progress or do you assume the original consent means everything is OK?

15. If you achieve consent once, do you assume it's always OK after that?

16. If someone consents to one thing, do you assume everything else is OK or do you ask before touching in different ways or taking things to more intense levels?

17. Are you resentful of people who need or want to talk about being abused? Why?

18. Are you usually attracted to people who fit the traditional standard of beauty as seen in the United States?

19. Do you pursue friendship with people because you want to be with them, and then give up on the friendship if that person isn't interested in you sexually?

20. Do you pursue someone sexually even after they have said they just want to be friends?

21. Do you assume that if someone is affectionate they are probably sexually interested in you?

22. Do you think about affection, sexuality, and boundaries? Do you talk about these issues with people? If so, do you talk about them only when you want to be sexual with someone or do you talk about them because you think it is important and you genuinely want to know?

23. Are you clear about your own intentions?

24. Have you ever tried to talk someone into doing something they showed hesitancy about?

25. Do you think hesitancy is a form of flirting?

26. If yes, are you aware that in some instances it is not?

27. Have you ever thought someone's actions were flirtatious when that wasn't actually the message they wanted to get across?

28. Do you think that if someone is promiscuous that makes it OK to objectify them or talk about them in ways you normally wouldn't?

29. If someone is promiscuous, do you think it's less important to get consent?

30. Do you think that if someone dresses in a certain way it makes it OK to objectify them?

31. If someone dresses a certain way do you think it means they want your sexual attention or approval?

32. Do you understand that there are many other reasons, that have nothing to do with you, that a person might want to dress or act in a way that you might find sexy?

33. Are you attracted to people with a certain kind of gender presentation?

34. Have you ever objectified someone's gender presentation?

35. Do you assume that each person who fits a certain perceived gender presentation will interact with you in the same way?

36. Do you think sex is a game?

37. Do you ever try to get yourself into situations that give you an excuse for touching someone you think would say "no" if you asked? i.e., dancing, getting really drunk around them, falling asleep next to them.

38. Do you make people feel "unfun" or "unliberated" if they don't want to try certain sexual things?

39. Do you think there are ways you act that might make someone feel that way even if it's not what you're trying to do?

40. Do you ever try and make bargains? i.e. "if you let me _____, I'll do_____ for you"?

41. Have you ever tried asking someone what they're feeling? If so, did you listen to them and respect them?

42. Have you used jealousy as a means of control?

43. Do you feel like being in a relationship with someone means that they have an obligation to have sex with you?

44. What if they want to abstain from sex for a week? A month? A year?

45. Do you whine or threaten if you're not having the amount of sex or the kind of sex that you want?

46. Do you think it's OK to initiate something sexual with someone who's sleeping?

47. What if the person is your partner?

48. Do you think it's important to talk with them about it when they're awake first?

49. Do you ever look at how you interact with people or how to treat people, positive or negative, and where that comes from or where you learned it?

50. Do you behave differently when you've been drinking?

51. What are positive aspects of drinking for you? What are negative aspects?

52. Have you been sexual with people when you were drunk or when they were drunk? Have you ever felt uncomfortable or embarrassed about it the next day? Has the person you were with ever acted weird to you afterward?

53. Do you seek consent the same way when you are drunk as when you're sober?

54. Do you think it is important to talk the next day with the person you've been sexual with if there has been drinking involved? If not, is it because it's uncomfortable or because you think something might have happened that shouldn't have? Or is it because you think that's just the way things go?

55. Do you think people need to take things more lightly?

56. Do you think these questions are repressive and people who look critically at their sexual histories and their current behavior are uptight and should be more "liberated"?

57. Do you think liberation might be different for different people?

58. Do you find yourself repeating binary gender behaviors, even within queer relationships and friendships? How might you doing this make others feel?

59. Do you view sexuality and gender presentation as part of a whole person, or do you consider those to be exclusively sexual aspects of people?

60. If someone is dressed in drag, do you take it as an invitation to make sexual comments?

61. Do you fetishize people because of their gender presentation?

62. Do you think only men abuse?

63. Do you think that in a relationship between people of the same gender, only the one who is more "manly" abuses?

64. How do you react if someone becomes uncomfortable with what you're doing or if they don't want to do something? Do you get defensive? Do you feel guilty? Does the other person end up having to take care of you and reassure you? Or are you able to step back and listen and hear them and support them and take responsibility for your actions?

65. Do you tell your side of the story and try and change the way they experienced the situation?

66. Do you do things to show your partner that you're listening and that you're interested in their ideas about consent or their ideas about what you did?

67. Do you ever talk about sex and consent when you're not in bed?

68. Have you ever raped or sexually abused or sexually manipulated someone? Are you able to think about your behavior? Have you made changes? What kinds of changes?

69. Are you uncomfortable with your body or your sexuality?

70. Have you been sexually abused?

71. Has your own discomfort or your own abuse history caused you to act in abusive ways? If so, have you ever been able to talk to anyone about it? Do you think talking about it is or could be helpful?

72. Do you avoid talking about consent or abuse because you aren't ready to or don't want to talk about your own sexual abuse history?

73. Do you ever feel obligated to have sex?

74. Do you ever feel obligated to initiate sex?

75. What if days, months, or years later someone tells you they were uncomfortable with what you did? Do you grill them?

76. Do you initiate conversations about safe sex and birth control (if applicable)?

77. Do you think that saying something as vague as "I've been tested recently" is enough?

78. Do you take your partners concerns about safe sex and/or birth control seriously?

79. Do you think that if one person wants to have safe sex and the other person doesn't really care, it is the responsibility of the person who has concerns to provide safe sex supplies?

80. Do you think if a person has a body that can get pregnant and they don't want to get pregnant, it is up to them to provide birth control?

81. Do you complain or refuse safe sex or the type of birth control your partner want to use because it reduces your pleasure?

82. Do you try and manipulate your partner about these issues?

83. Do you think there is ongoing work that we can do to end sexual violence in our communities?

Good Guy

Anonymous

One girlfriend I had, her previous boyfriend used to beat her up. I was clueless, cruel, cold-hearted, and eighteen. I think she loved me because I didn't hit her. I wasn't very kind otherwise.

The next girlfriend I had told me she wasn't into blowjobs because she used to have to give them to her uncle. We often had sex with our clothes on. The last six months of our relationship we had sex twice. I didn't know how to process the information about her and her uncle. Somehow I knew it wasn't unusual, and I guess having clear parameters (no blowjobs) made it an easy thing for me to avoid and still feel like I was doing alright by her.

A few years later I got very drunk at a house show. I ran into a friend there and she gave me a ride back to her house. We made out and then she undressed me and we had sex. I didn't want to, but I was drunk and something said that, as a guy, I shouldn't feel uncomfortable. My body was reacting, but I felt terrible and something in my head told me it was weak to say no.

The next day we went to an amusement park and sat on a bench. I threw up in the garbage can repeatedly. She took me home. I was very hungover, and disgusted with both myself and her. I knew it wasn't the biggest thing—so minor compared to what every woman I'd had a relationship with had experienced. I was mad at myself for getting into that situation with an old friend. I kept telling myself it wasn't that big a deal, but I left town for two weeks without telling anyone.

It was awhile before I had any kind of sexual contact with anyone again.

With the next girlfriend, things went very slow.

When I think about what it might mean to be a good partner to someone, I think of her. The way she talked about her own experiences and talked to me about mine. "Is this OK?" "Why does this feel weird?" I didn't tell her at first, but she kept asking in a way that was gentle and patient. It seemed seamless.

I still don't get it, but I'm more careful than I used to be, I'm more aware. I'm used to being seen as a good guy or (lord forbid) a sensitive guy, but I know that in reality it hasn't added up to shit because other people's abuse was something I had to negotiate. I never went out of my way to understand it or deal with it until my own boundaries were crossed in such a minor way.

Frozen Inside

Cindy Crabb

I can't believe how it keeps happening; people waking up to someone they know touching them. How the hell can anyone think it is OK to initiate sex with someone who is sleeping? Do they think about our abuse histories? Or the fact that we can't say "no" when we're asleep? Do they understand our complex defense systems and how vulnerable and terrified we might feel waking up to this assault? Do they know that even if we go along with it all once we wake up, it doesn't necessarily mean we want to? We have complex ways of protecting ourselves. Do they think about this?

The truth is, I used to crawl into people's beds too. I thought it was OK. I thought of course all guys wanted it. I never considered the fact that I might be capable of assault, but of course, I am. A lot of us are.

Are you seeing this? Will you promise to take steps to never do it again? (Like don't get in bed with someone when you're wasted or unsure about your intentions. Stop making excuses for yourself. Look at your life for real.)

I am sick of how it all keeps happening. I can't stand how often people tell me something like this: "I told him early in the night that just because we were getting drunk together didn't mean I want to fuck him. I specifically said 'I don't want to have sex with you' and then later, he was just on me. Do we call this rape?"

Or how many times I've heard "I didn't say 'no' outright, but I tried to make it clear." Then there are all the times we try to comfort someone or find comfort in their arms, and they think it's an invitation to do what they want. We trust people and they don't understand (or care?) about the difference between emotional openness and sexual desire. Or how it happens; if we're slutty or flirty, people think we're open game. If we're shy they think it's a form of flirt and really they just need to be persistent in pressuring us. This game is not always a fun game for all of us.

Yesterday a tough girl friend of mine said "I have not had consensual sex all year." The day before I heard friends laughing about two people we knew who had been wrestling and one of them had just though it was comradery until the other person... And everyone is laughing at the story because it is a boy-boy story, which I don't think is funny at all.

The day before, I had been reading a zine where the author called someone out. She says "That was assault, asshole!" but at the end of the page it says, "I should have fought."

I am sick of people saying, "Well if you didn't want it, why didn't you say something? I never would have had sex (or whatever) if I'd known."

I am sick of the blame and self-blame. We have had practically everything taken away from us and cannot always speak. And what kind of world are we building if it's still seen as our responsibility to say something? Why isn't it their responsibility to ask and to watch for signs and signals and ask again?

You know how there are supposedly two instinctual responses— fight or flight? Well there's also freeze. You can see it everywhere in nature, especially in animals that are under constant attack.

A friend of mine tells me about this. She says "frozen, the soul can go somewhere where it won't be touched. Frozen, maybe the cougar will just pass it by. Frozen, if it does get killed it doesn't hurt as much."

I laugh, nervous laugh, because do I believe in a soul? Plus, it always hurt pretty bad the times I've been assaulted and/or raped while frozen.

My friend says "One of the differences between us and the deer is that once the danger is past, the deer finds their family and then they shake and shake, get the trauma out of their bodies, somewhere safe, with the protective family around. Where do we get that release and support?"

"At the punk show." I say

"Come on now, really," she says. And of course, it is not true. It is not the same. She says "We don't get support and release. We are almost never in a place of safety. The trauma builds in us. We freeze our voices, our bodies. We become frozen inside."

She thinks it is instinct and culture. I think it is systematic oppression and patriarchy. But sometimes, now alone in my room, I shake and I shake and I scream.

Am I Safe?

I never thought I'd feel safe enough to just lay around all sleepy at a party like this.

Bla bla bla

bla bla

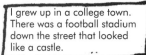

I didn't always feel so safe...

I grew up in a college town. There was a football stadium down the street that looked like a castle.

We were kids and we'd go to parties. There was always something about these parties that made me uneasy...

...like I was surrounded by predators

This is the capitol building in the town where I'm from. I just wanted to include it in the comic because it sort of exemplifies the mentality of the town as a whole.

There was a strip of bars beside my house where the frat boys would get their girlfriends drunk.

The girls would be out on the porches in the dead of winter with high heels + short skirts + I would roll my eyes as I passed.

But now I just want to walk up to them, say something wise or empowering. Tell them it doesn't have to be this way.

But I don't have much to offer, really. I used to try and play that game too.

And I've been really fucking lucky.

I chalk it up to a series of narrow escapes.

Blacked out on the side of the road later that evening

There were so many nights spent this way, head spinning, wondering why.

Why!

Why do I feel the constant threat of danger? My heart is pounding by the time I reach the door. Where does this fear come from?

And why do I bring the fear home with me where I cower in the corner feeling powerless, worthless, + alone?

And why do the boys at these parties want me to lose consciousness? Why don't they want me awake to see them with clear + open eyes?

And why do I even go to these parties? Why do I feel compelled to take part in the game?

Where am I? Am I safe? Oh yes, I remember. I'm watching the brass band. Safe.

At last... I think I'm safe. I want to be...

NO MEANS NO

"Consent Matters"

"NOT NOW" MEANS **NO**

I HAVE A BOY/GYRLFRIEND MEANS **NO**

MAYBE LATER MEANS **NO**

YOU'RE NOT MY TYPE MEANS **NO**

FUCK OFF MEANS **NO**

I'D RATHER BE ALONE RIGHT NOW MEANS **NO**

DON'T TOUCH ME MEANS **NO**

I REALLY LIKE YOU BUT... MEANS **NO**

LET'S JUST GO TO SLEEP MEANS **NO**

I'M NOT SURE MEANS **NO**

YOU/I'VE BEEN DRINKING MEANS **NO**

SILENCE MEANS **NO**

DATE RAPE = **NOT** UNDERSTANDING **NO**

Activism and Survival

By S.H.

I haven't thought about any of this stuff consciously in a long while, have spent the last five years trying to stuff it under the surface. After ten years of therapy, I can only say that "something bad" happened with an older male family member. In my twenties I tried to pull at those threads and unravel them, and I had terrible panic attacks and depression on and off for years. My family disowned me and I caved. Now I am living a split life, in contact with my family and pretending nothing happened while knowing inside that it did. After that early experience, I got into many other bad situations with men because I was so numbed out and unaware that I could *want* anything.

What's always hurt me is that I wanted to do political organizing around women's issues and never could. It's mysterious, but being with a group of women always triggers me, because something about rape or assault will come up and I'll feel for a few days like I'm drowning and I can't breathe. I have responded to the whole sexual assault thing by being very tough and no-nonsense in my activist and job lives, and being with women makes me feel things, makes me feel vulnerable and then I feel crazy because I lose control. It's weird, I have wanted more than anything to be politically active with a group of women, but because I want it so much, I get intimidated when I get near real women I admire. If I don't have a sense that they've gone through something similar, I get afraid they will reject me for being damaged, and if they *have* been through something similar, I get afraid they'll talk about it too much and I'll get triggered. I don't know, my relationships with women are fulfilling but complicated, I think partially because my mom "sold me out" on numerous occasions and chose the abuser over me.

Being assaulted has taken a lot from me. I get triggered all the time and have one thousand tricks that no one knows for keeping it together. Even at activist conferences, there are creepy men and

I find myself panicking and being defensive and silent instead of speaking up and telling them to get the fuck away. I had EMDR [Eye Movement Desensitization and Reprocessing] treatment a few years ago, which really helped and has taken some of the edge off my startle reflex.

This *is* political. I always forget that, or I know it for other people but not for me.

Having been assaulted means I have a fucked up relationship to activism sometimes. I take on too much and say yes to too much because I think I'm not worthy or even alive unless I'm in pain and panicked and doing too much for other people.

Being an assault survivor in a movement of anarcho-socialists and socialists is a weird thing. For example, people gave me weird looks when I got married and took my partner's last name, like "Ooh, you sell-out!" Screw that! I could explain to almost no one that I was overjoyed to get rid of the last name that linked me to my abuser. I just went from one man's name to another, and at least I love my husband. I think even in movements that call themselves radical, there are a lot of judgments about women and a total lack of understanding about what real women have to do to make it through the day.

This has also gotten *really* bizarre and important since I found out that I'm going to be the mom of a boy. I tried to admit to some movement people that it was a weird thing for me, but they looked at me like I was being vicious. I think for any feminist, the challenge of raising a *good* man is daunting and mysterious. For a sexual assault survivor, it is… well, for me at least it's alternately hopeful and very scary. It's a huge and beautiful challenge that might give me the first experience of loving a male completely and safely and unconditionally. I doubt my own abilities and I don't want to look at my son ever when I'm triggered or down on men and make him feel like I hate him just because he has a penis. But I will NOT raise him to be one of those smug shitters who is so "I'm a feminist" that he never listens and can never be wrong. I've seen more of those, including "radical" ones, than I've met decent radical men. One of the reasons I'm really into my husband is because he's a normal working class guy who knows men can be fucked up, not a holier-than-thou radical who wants to lecture me on being more "strong" or "feminist."

I feel like I've been working so hard for years to rise above this stuff and build a life and stay alive. That's my weird secret, because I tell almost no one these days. But it is *so* important to talk about and acknowledge and to give myself credit for dealing with it. Hopefully someday there will be a way to express this stuff out in the open. Thank you for letting in some air.

The Thing After

Shannon Parez-Darby

I have this muscle memory of distrust. My first instinct is to pull away; it's to push you away. I want to distrust you, I want you to push a little further because that's familiar because, "the devil you know is better than the devil you don't..." I want to learn how to do it differently. I want to teach my body another way of being. For me all of this learning, sex, relationships, abuse, power, crossed boundaries, panic attacks, and anxiety lives inside my body. My body reacts from its memory, from the ways it has learned to be.

So how do I do it differently? I work at a domestic violence organization and my job is essentially to talk about relationships. My job is healing and triggering all at once. When I think back to crossed boundaries, to consent, to the moments I've been asked about what I want, how I want to be touched and how I don't want to be touched my answer is silence more often than not.

You can ask for consent, be willing to hear yes and no, you can be engaged and present but if I'm too hurt to sit with you, to sit in my body with my responses and feelings, then where does that leave me? When I think about accountability and consent I think about all the ways I've learned to go along with it, to make things easy and to not make waves. There are so many moments when it's easier to say nothing, to not have to speak up or define my edges for you and I get to hide in the blurriness. It feels less scary to say nothing and pick up the pieces inside of myself than say no and have to discover where I start and you stop. I get lost in the messy places between us; that's not love and that's not accountability. For me accountability is showing up with my whole self, it's being present and brave enough to actually be somewhere with someone instead of hiding in my own insecurities, fear, and internalized shit. I want to do better than hiding.

As someone who mostly has sex with other folks socialized as girls, communication around consent in my life and communities is different than how I was taught growing up. For me, being a homo has meant a shift in how I understand my role when it comes to sex. When I was younger I was less of an active participant in the sex I was having and more of a referee. I never said "touch me here" or "I like it like this" but instead let whatever boy I was kissing do whatever he thought was sexy and my job was to make sure it never went too far over the (my) line. I was a gatekeeper always guarding whatever felt like the most vulnerable part of myself. Generally, by the time I was willing to use my voice we were several steps ahead of where I actually wanted to be. I would wait until the scales tipped, until whatever sexy place we were going was scarier than saying stop.

When I think about these interactions I'm filled with all of these contradictory things. I would call some of these experiences coercive and I struggle with that language of it all of the time. These are the moments when accountability feels muddled. I believe the guys I was having sex with were doing the best they could. I believe that they wanted to have mutually pleasurable sex and that they wished the best for me. It doesn't feel like an answer to say that they were all jerks or "evil perpetrators" that I then get to demonize. I believe that the men I was being sexy with had some pretty shitty skills and fucked up expectations and they didn't know how to do it better, which doesn't mean that they shouldn't be thoughtful about and accountable for their actions, but they also shouldn't be demonized for them either. When we make people evil it dehumanizes everyone.

I'm not sure how much energy it makes sense to put into this idea because then again I'm centering on them and their experiences and not mine. But I do want to push my communities to look at community accountability models. I'm not sure we have all of the skills to be enacting sustainable accountability models right now but I think we can be talking more about sexual assault within our own radical communities and how we extend the values of community, social justice, and anti-oppression into our conversations around consent and accountability.

Saying that I don't want to demonize the people who have been sexually coercive in my life has become easier because, for the most part, these interactions are far away; they're in the past and none of these guys are in my life anymore. We were working off of this hetero script that says that guys are the drivers, they will go as far as they can with a girl and it's the girls job to be the brakes, always guarding against men who will try to get as much as they can around sex from her unless she puts a stop to it. This script is a setup for everyone. It's a setup for the guys because there is no space to have a full range of emotions, to not want to have sex or to feel anything other than sex crazed, always looking for and wanting sex. It's a setup for women because whatever happens is our fault; either we don't say anything and silence is consent, or we speak up and we are troublemakers or prudes.

I don't want to set up a false dichotomy that straight men are inherently coercive and queers are radical and thus have only equitable (sexual) relationships because that's not true, and that idea is getting in the way of creating communities that are looking at and engaging with a process of accountability. Homos protect the fucked up things we do to each other and it's scary to talk about because what if that proves all of the fucked up things homophobic society says about us? What if we can't have equitable relationships? What if all of this work we're doing to create the kinds of relationships we want for ourselves isn't working? Not talking about this is not keeping us safe; it's keeping us isolated and it's making sure that we perpetuate the same shitty coercive dynamics that we have learned. It means that when coercion and sexual assault happen in our queer communities we don't talk about it, we internalize our oppression and we stay hidden.

I want more models for the relationships and the kinds of sex I want to be having in my life. Sometimes the queers I know pretend that we're more radical than coercion and abuse, that this stuff doesn't affect us, that it doesn't seep into our sex lives and relationships. Pretending that I'm more "down" than you, that I'm more radical and liberated reinforces the same stuff I'm trying to unlearn. It makes us feel like we are not enough. I'm tired of us all feeling like we're not OK. What would it look like to believe that we could do it another way, that we could do it a million other ways? What would our sexual interactions look like if we believed that we were OK, if we were allowed to be our whole selves, if we saw ourselves as whole? What would it look like to be able to sit with our fears and engage in a process of accountability with each other? What if we were able to show up in a centered, solid, whole, and grace-filled way? What would accountability look like? What would we need to even imagine this?

The scariest thing I can think to say to someone I'm dating is that I don't want to have sex. What does my accountability process look like around this? What does consent look like when I'm not even sure I could tell you no? I don't think this is the most loving way I can show up. When our scripts shift and I'm the one touching you, I'm initiating sex and I'm no longer the brakes but actively engaged, what does consent look like then? All of a sudden my responsibility shifts. I've trained myself to go with the flow, and now I have a more equitable role in asking how you like to be touched, how you don't want to be touched, what's too light and what's not hard enough and not just once but all the time. It's a constant process of engagement. When I look at this power shift, I see it's a re-envisioning of the sex I had when I was younger. I can feel the complexity and layers of how we learn to treat each other. You can have someone's best intentions in mind but that doesn't mean that you won't fuck up. That's the scariest thing: sometimes when it comes to crossing someone's boundaries it doesn't matter where your heart is. We can be trying our best and still cross each other's boundaries. That's not to say that intention isn't important. Intention sometimes makes the difference in my healing process, but my experience has mostly been that I can't really know what's happening for other folks. We have a lot invested in seeing people that perpetrate sexual assault as evil villains and seeing people that are surviving sexual assault as perfect angels. This narrative hurts us all because it's not about good or evil but about power. Often we get power without asking for it, and giving power away can feel counterintuitive because it's something we're not taught to do and have almost no models for. Mostly people who have power and privilege don't necessarily feel like they do. So if coercion is generally about power and most people that have power don't feel like they do, then where does that leave us when we're trying to negotiate sex? When we're talking about consent; how to say yes and no? How do we know when we have the power? How do we figure out how to shift power dynamics and what do we do when we use our power (intentionally or not) in fucked up ways? How do we hear and respond when someone says they're not feeling heard or that they feel like their lines have been crossed? How do we honor what an amazing thing it is that someone is even able to say that at all?

Accountability is a process, and part of that process is screwing up. That's so scary and so real because, when the stakes are this high, screwing up doesn't really feel like an option. What if instead we see accountability as a process we get to engage with when we fuck up. Fucking up is going to happen. Instead of denial and hiding, instead of saying that we didn't know any better (whether that's true or not) we can apologize, figure out what is up for us, what places inside of us our actions are centered and then figure out what we're going to do about it. Because screwing up is a part of the deal, but that doesn't mean we get to fuck up in the same way over and over again. We engage so we don't keep fucking up in the exact same ways. I want to discover the totally new way I'm going to mess up.

In order to do this we have to be coming from a place where we assume that people are trying their hardest and where people really are trying their hardest. Because the reality is that people do really shitty things to each other and, frankly, I don't always know how to make sense of that. As a survivor of abuse, as a domestic violence advocate, as a friend and a person in community with other people, I've seen and heard some of the really shitty awful things that people do to each other. At work, folks call us all the time with really heavy hard stories and those are true and real and everyone makes sense of their experiences and finds healing in ways that are real for them. Healing is a process more than something we achieve once and for all.

Accountability is not taking all of the responsibility and apologizing forever. We all know the script; someone screws up and when they're called out their response is, "It's all my fault, how could I do this, I am a terrible person, how could you even like me?" So then I'm comforting you or you're comforting me when really I should be apologizing for messing up. It's a way of looking like we're being accountable without actually having to apologize and look at our actions. Sometimes this looks like accountability but really it's a mask that keeps us from sitting with ourselves and getting real about what's going on inside of us.

I choose to believe that the people in my life are doing the best they can. That doesn't mean that they get to treat me badly or do shitty things. Holding this complexity has often been very painful, jumping from unearned trust in people who keep crossing my boundaries and not respecting me, to martyrdom where someone fucks up and I keep throwing myself into the fire saying, "they're doing the best they can." I believe there can be a place in between, a place where I can be real with myself and present for the constant engagement it takes to be good to the people in my life and demand respect and kindness.

patterns

Anonymous

I was raised to believe that guys wanted sex all the time, and that if they didn't get off when they were turned on, then they'd get blue-balls, which was totally painful and terrible. I was raised to believe that it was my job to do what was needed. I was abused when I was young, and then dated much older guys, but when I was eighteen I was in a relationship with someone my age. One time when he was out of town I read his journal (which, needless to say, was a really terribly wrong thing to do). In the journal it said something about how tired he was of always having to have sex with me in the mornings. The thing was, I didn't want to have sex either. I thought because he was hard, that meant I had to do it, and so I would initiate. I generally initiated when I thought someone wanted it so that I wouldn't have to try and say no, and then be raped (even though this boy would have never ever raped me and I knew that). Reading his journal was the first time I realized that *I* could be the one who had power, and that *I* could be coercive even when I didn't want to be. This led me to really commit myself to reading about childhood sexual abuse and, of course, it was a long task. I am still learning.

For me, it is important to be really conscious, but sometimes I can fall into old patterns when I least expect it. For a while, polyamory was really important for me in trying to figure out my own sexuality and how to have healthy relationships. Sometimes I was good at it and sometimes I used polyamory as an excuse to be dismissive of other people's feelings and needs. Reading Wendy-O Matik's book, *Redefining Our Relationships*, was really useful in helping me figure out how to be ethical in my polyamory and not just use it as a holier-than-thou manipulation tactic. Eventually I decided polyamory fed into my over-sexualization of everyone I knew, and that I didn't want to be thinking that way about everyone. I wanted to be able to have clear friendships and clear boundaries. It was good for me to stop flirting and to figure out ways to connect with my friends that weren't sexual. I started to form much closer and more stable relationships with my friends, which has helped me learn about setting boundaries and respecting boundaries in all areas of my life.

I still struggle with always turning closeness into sexual feelings. I don't really blame myself for it, because I know that it comes from childhood abuse. I am trying to learn ways to be really upfront with my friends when I am trying to get physical, non-sexual comfort. I've found that even when it seems obvious, it's completely important to me to state from the beginning, "I want to cuddle but don't want to do anything sexual," even when it's with my best friend and I have said it a hundred times before. I just almost always think that when someone touches me they want to have sex, and then I start responding to this assumed want. So stating what we are doing beforehand helps.

There have been a couple times recently when I have been sleeping next to a new friend, feeling quite certain that we wouldn't do anything, and then ended up doing sexual stuff that felt consensual. In both cases I knew I should have talked about it as it was happening, and in both cases, I was older and felt like it was my responsibility to bring it up, but I try not to beat myself up about it and have made sure to talk to them later to make sure it was OK. These talks went really well.

For My Father...

Jake Holloway

Last time I saw my father, he sat across from me at dinner and told me about the face of the monster that would appear to him out of nowhere when he tried to sleep at night. It was horrible, half-eaten face of a dog, all fangs and teeth and ripped flesh. It would loom over him in the dark.

My father's stories. They would cling to me like tiny shards of glass. He would toss them to me over breakfast. Sweep them under my feet on the back porch. Offer them up in our crowded family car and I would choke on tobacco smoke and the burden of too many splintered memories swallowed whole.

He stopped drinking when I was eleven. When you stop drinking, there are one or two years of bliss. Effortless life. The exhilaration of clear vision and shaky, nervous fingers. They call this the honeymoon period. And then all at once, the darkness melts away and all those terrible stories you tried to obscure blossom into sharp and distinct forms, gleaming teeth and broken edges.

This is when the memories of my grandmother began to surface.

I don't know details really.

I don't want to.

When her second husband died, she took my father into her bedroom and told him that he was the man of the house.

I am sitting in the back seat of the car. I only want to hear the music on the radio.

My grandmother's eyes are small and glowing like glass beads. She is young for her age. Her ankles are thin and fragile like mine. She is still very much alive despite her catheter and sunken cheeks. I wait patiently by her bed. I feed her Jell-O while my father paces the halls. She is dripping like a wilted flower. She reveals herself—all folded flesh and blue veins, her colostomy bag spilling along the white linoleum. I watch her struggle, humiliated and stunned by her own fading life.

I watch my father and his boyish terror.

I watch my own eyes in the mirror of the house I grew up in. I look for pieces of her shimmering in my quivering lips and my broken gaze.

I don't want this woman to exist inside my skin, dendrites tracing paths forged by her.

I don't want to know.

My father was raped on Neptune Beach. He'd been looking for perfect conch shells without missing pieces.

Some man asked my father if he wanted to go on a ride.

He took my father to a hotel room and held a blade to his throat.

My father lived with a man once, a composer named Jonathon. They lived together for ten years. This was before he met my mother.

My father was a young, promising actor. He and Jonathon drank together and wrote songs. Brilliant songs.

This man feared fame more than life. He locked himself in a cheap hotel the night his play made it onto Broadway.

He died recently. He'd been living in a one-bedroom apartment in a housing project in South Georgia. He was studying the Roman Empire and the music of Croatia.

My father always had ways of escaping, even when he was small. He would run out to the trapeze in the backyard. He would swing skyward and sail above barns and red clay, chicken bones, threadbare tires, shotgun shells, bits of china gleaming under a godlike southern sun. He would swing up and up and up.

He would go to the movies on Saturdays and disappear into silvery California moonlight, floor-length satin gowns; swelling violins. Romance and cowboys and men in velvet waistcoats. Marilyn Monroe! My father knew he could save her from the pills and the pain of stardom. He wrote her letters and her press agent sent him an autographed photo that he kept under his pillow.

Oh god, these stories pile up around my brittle ankles, sink into my skin.

There was the stark, swollen grip of the drunk who married his mother. He would chase them outside in the dead of night with a rifle in his hand, firing shots that sank into the flaccid soil of the cotton fields. He would read my father's fortune in coffee grounds. He would toss empty bottles at the wall.

And one day he draped his hands over my father's shoulders and his hands were like buckets of moonshine, heavy and damp and spilling over the edge. And this man, this man who wandered through the house like a pixilated beast, who tossed china out of doorways and shattered windows, this man looked deep into my father's already frantic eyes and said, "You are my son."

I have always known that I am my father's daughter. I can tell by the way I twist little pieces of paper into spirals between my fingers. I can tell by the way darkness wraps around my brain like a raincoat. I can hear his nervous laugh rattling in my ribcage. We both have trouble breathing while we sleep.

My veins are swollen and heavy with thick blood. I am carrying memories that are not mine. My cells are saturated with secrets. I am listening to stories whispered across the table, through closed doors, over the back seat.

I don't want to know.

I don't want to know.

I only want to hear the music on the radio.

Denial

Anonymous

I didn't realize the complexities of denial. I never knew that it could possess layers upon layers of its own truth. I didn't comprehend that denial could have its own purpose beyond what I could understand. Mostly, I didn't know that denial was my protection.

I'm not even talking about the denial that saved me as a child: all families are like mine, my mom loves me, things aren't so bad, things could be worse. No, I'm talking about the denial I've had in my healing process. A lot of it was the same mantras as before, but in a different context: piece of cake, I can get over this standing on my head. It wasn't so horrible, I'm still alive. It wasn't so horrible, I'm not in an institution. It wasn't so bad, I haven't tried to kill myself in years. I'm making such a big deal out of nothing. After all, everyone gets depressed, everyone is suicidal.

So why do I say denial was a good thing? Because it saved me from having to take the full weight of what has happened to me all at once.

I still have my moments of denial, and maybe I will for the rest of my life, but for the most part, it's gone. At its height, I couldn't wish it away fast enough. I just wanted to be sure. I wanted to believe my memories 150% without a doubt. Now that I do, I am often plagued by something more difficult to deal with than denial; sadness. For if I believe fully in the memories I have uncovered, then I must believe those memories are true and real. And if I believe they are true, then I must accept that they really happened to me.

Sadness feels weird. Depression, I know like the back of my hand. Depression comes in big waves, and it's a struggle just to get out of bed. Eventually it ends. Sadness is different. It comes and goes. I never see it until it is right in front of me. Sleep won't make it go away. There is no "anti-sadness" medication on the market. It's not debilitating, it's just an all-body experience, like a sigh from the bottom of me that just keeps coming out. I never know when I'll get to take in another breath.

Healing, like denial, is multi-layered. It's important to have tunnel vision, to constantly remember that all of this is leading toward a brighter place. The thing is, healing doesn't always feel like healing. Sometimes it just hurts. In those moments, looking for a better place seems like denial itself. Maybe it is, and maybe that's why it works.

Frozen Inside #2

Cindy Crabb

Maybe we need a hundred new words for when our friends or acquaintances or partners assault or rape us. One word to describe "I let you because I was half asleep and too tired to do anything else." One that's "I was sick of arguing about it." One for "It's fucked up and scary the way you talk to me." One for "I told you I didn't want to do that." One for "Why didn't you notice when I wasn't present anymore." One for "We had an agreement you'd use protection." One for "You said if I didn't do it, you'd leave me. What choice did I have?"

Maybe we need a hundred new words to talk about rape and sexual assault and sexual manipulation: words that speak clearly about the seriousness of what is being done to our bodies. Or maybe our friends and acquaintances and partners need to have the courage to hear "You raped me" or "That was assault." (I still barely ever use these words because I know the backlash consequences. I know that no one has the courage to hear their actions defined that way. They don't want to admit they are capable of rape or assault. They don't want to admit that patriarchy exists and that it gives them the God- and State-granted right to do these things. They don't want to look at the political and physical nature of their actions. They want to blow it all off. They have a million reasons for what they did.)

Every time I've tried to talk with someone about the sexual stuff that they did to me that I didn't want, their first reaction is to (usually frantically) try to explain it away. They want the story to be different than the one I am telling. They want me to see it through *their* eyes and absolve them. They say "But I thought...," they say "I never would have...," even "No, that's not what happened!" (As if their experience was the only one.) They try to make me out as crazy. They say I am blaming them for things that are really just stored up from my past.

I am not crazy. I am aware that capitalism and patriarchy and all systems of control depend on the denial of both the oppressor and the oppressed. I know that patriarchy values logic over emotion and that "too much" emotion, too strong a response, will get you labeled crazy, and that women and people on the female spectrum are considered to be crazy a lot of the time. We are not crazy. What happens to us is real. All the attempts to silence us won't change this reality.

I carry with me a whole history of sexual abuse, and so do most of us. Each sexual act does not exist in a vacuum and I'm sick of people treating it as if it does. I never again want to hear the words, "Well, why didn't you stop me?" I want to hear, "Oh my god! I am so sorry!," and then I want them to ask for my story. I want them to be able to take it instead of asking for pity. If I tell them to fuck off and leave me alone, then I want them to respect that. If it's someone I love, I might want them to hold me so I can cry. If it's someone I hate, I want to be able to punch them without the community saying "That's so fucked up! She hit him!"

I want all of them to say "I believe you. I'm taking this seriously. I hate what I've done and I'm going to change. I'm going to commit myself (or recommit myself) to looking deep inside of myself and changing my behavior and looking at this world and what it's made me into, and it's my responsibility. I'm going to take this seriously. Thank you for having the courage to tell me. I'm going to work as hard as possible to make sure I never do that to anyone ever again."

I want them to say that and feel it, and mean it, and follow through.

letter

Dear Cindy,

... I read your column for *Slug and Lettuce*. Oh, I love the way it is angry and questioning, very direct and clear in the anger. Yeah, I was at Nove Miasto and asked some of the guys there to read it, and they complained about how small the print was so I went and photocopied it BIG and then they didn't have any excuses. But let's not talk about excuses. I am glad that you wrote such a moving piece, it makes me feel OK when I've been questioning lately how I "let" certain situations happen. But fuck that! I have been so conditioned, trained, and taught my entire life that whatever he says goes, and that it is more important to be sexy and liked by the guys than building lasting honest relationships with people...

I've been thinking and writing about all these situations/stories from my life that have reinforced a patriarch deep within my head, and it's really making me split wide open as I start to understand where it's been coming from and how I perpetuate it. It's exciting, kinda; I can see how I am moving away from it and challenging behaviors that wreck me. And maybe also, I'm just over it. Maybe I'm finally realizing that being boy-crazy ain't where it's at. That random fucking hurts and leaves me bruised, and that no kinda boyfriend/soulmate/partner will complete me and provide my happiness. In some ways it seems like so much work to break out of these patterns, but I'm also feeling a big sense of relief and excitement at letting it go...

Love, Sarah

PART 2

Healing and Transforming Ourselves

Let's Talk about Consent

Consent Matters

Here are some ways to ask in the heat of the moment. But don't forget, talking about it when you're not half naked is always better.

    May I:

              touch_____?
              kiss _____?
              put my _____?

Are you into this?
How are you feeling?
What would you like me to do?
I think it's hot when my partner does _____ to me?
What do you like?
Would you like it if I_____?
Where do you see this going?
What should I look for if you start to shut down?

How do you define consent? Write it down and keep it in your pocket.

Write a list of your goals for future sex and then write how to achieve them. Keep it in your pocket.

Write a list of your current boundaries. Keep it in your pocket.

Sex

Cindy Crabb

"Nearly all the survivors I have worked with report having had sex when they didn't want to. It's almost as if this were taken for granted; unwanted sex becomes such a given for survivors that many hardly notice it anymore."
—Staci Haines, *The Survivors Guide to Sex: How to Have an Empowered Sex Life After Child Sexual Abuse*

"Sometimes there are a number of seemingly contradictory feelings happening in your body at once. You may feel sexually turned on in your hips and vulva, and feel pulled away in your chest...What do you do then? Actually, experiencing contradictory feelings is familiar territory for most survivors. Consent then becomes a matter of distinguishing what sensations are what."
— Staci Haines, *The Survivors Guide to Sex*

"Survivors are not alone in needing to heal sexually. Our culture leaves little room for people to develop healthy, integrated sexuality. Almost from birth, girls are given mixed messages about their sexuality. They are alternately told to hide it, deny it, repress it, use it, or give it away. The media flaunt sex constantly as a means of power, seduction and exchange. As a result, most women grow up with conflicts around sex. For women who were abused, these problems are compounded."
—Ellen Bass and Laura Davis, *The Courage to Heal: A Guide for Women Survivors of Child Sexual Abuse*

Talking about sex can be really hard—when were we ever taught to talk about it? What language do we use? How do we *not* feel embarrassed? But really, it is our bodies, it is our lives, it is something that's supposed to be cool and fun and amazing, and why shouldn't we talk about it?

It shouldn't be the responsibility of the person who was abused to initiate conversations about sex.

Spacing out and flashbacks: talking can help. If they looks like they're[1] not present, ask. You could ask them to open their eyes (don't demand it, just say something like "I wish I could see your eyes," or "are you there?"). Sometimes just a voice can bring us back. Sometimes not. It is good to stop or slow down if you are not sure where they are. Sometimes you can come up with a code word, like "ghosts" because some people cannot say stop and cannot express what's going on. Please don't overreact. Don't press them for information. Don't feel inadequate. What is appropriate will vary. Sometimes they may want you to leave them alone. Sometimes they may want to stay with the flashback and open it up so they can gain information about the past. Sometimes they will want to be in the present.

You can talk about what kind of help they might need to stay present. Maybe they need to say out loud "I want to be in the present." Maybe they need you to say their name or your name, or maybe to tell a story of something simple and nice, not sex related, that you've done together lately. The spiral down can make us forget that there were ever nice, simple times or any feelings other than fear and helplessness.

When things come up, it can be really important to talk about them again when you're not in bed. You can say "I know you couldn't talk about what was making you so scared and sad last night, but I do really care and really want to know. Do you think you can talk about it now?" Maybe they'll say yes, maybe they'll say no. You can say "It was confusing when I asked if you were OK and you said 'I'm fine' but you didn't really sound fine and I didn't know what to do. What should I do when that happens?" Maybe they'll say—yeah, they actually were fine, just trying to bring themselves back into the present and they were glad you didn't stop and that you trusted them. Maybe they'll say—yeah, actually they were saying "fine" to be cynical, and they're glad you noticed, glad you stopped.

You can say, "do you like it when I_____? I can't tell." Maybe they'll say, "I want to like it but it makes me feel weird." Maybe they'll say, "It's triggering, but I'm trying to work through that trigger." Maybe they'll say, "I don't really like that, but I didn't know how to say anything."

---

1   "They" refers to a gender non-specific singular person, not multiple people.

If you're courting someone, sleeping with someone, thinking of getting in a relationship with someone, always assume that they could have been sexually abused. Know that for many sexual abuse survivors—even ones who love sex and are aggressively sexual—there will very likely be a period of time when they don't want to have sex. Think about whether you are willing or able to be in a committed relationship that isn't sexual. It is totally sucky to be an abuse survivor, be emotionally dependent on someone, be having a time of serious abuse triggers, try to set boundaries, try to say you don't want to have sex for a while, and then have that person freak out or threaten to leave you. If you are willing to be in a relationship that isn't always sexual (even if you love sex), then it could be a good thing to remind the one you love that if they ever don't want to have sex, it's totally OK.

Every abuse survivor has different needs. They may want to touch you but not be touched. They may want to be touched but not touch you. They may want to have really wild sex. The may want to start over and learn to just make out without going all the way. And everything may change at any given moment.

> "Your experience of sex can change within a single relationship... With a new lover, there's often a passionate rush that obscures problems. But as the relationship settles, sexual issues may need attention again. As you risk more emotional intimacy, you may start to shut down sexually. Or you may find that as your trust grows and deepens, you heal on a deep body level, surpassing even your own expectations.
> Because it takes a long time to heal sexually, you may wonder whether you're making progress. But even though the process has ups and downs, you are headed in the right direction. If you are putting steady, consistent effort into developing a fulfilling sexuality, have patience, accept where you are, and trust your capacity to heal."
> —Ellen Bass and Laura Davis, *The Courage to Heal*

Unsolicited Advice Column

Anandi Wonder

I want to talk about what I see coming up in our lives so often, which are casual encounters. For example, maybe you guys are drunk and you start making out at a party. Or you've been flirting for a while and go on a date and finally start making out. What I mean is, you don't really know each other super well yet, and it's just not time for the big talk, you know? Like, maybe after, or next time, you'll start talking and tell each other things about your histories or whatever, but by then it might be too late; you might've already totally freaked this person out by unknowingly acting like a total dick.

Some stuff should be obvious. If someone says, "I don't want to be sexual," and then you put your hand in their pants while they're asleep, well… you're a creep, and you're not even trying to not be one. But! I think even the biggest creeps can change! I'm going to assume that the majority of people reading this are good people, and that if you're making out with someone, it's meant to be fun for both of you, you want them to be happy, you don't want to cause them pain. So I'm going to try to help you, so no one need ever say again, "I didn't know! How could I have?" It's never too late to start being awesome.

If you think you have never been with someone with a history of abuse or rape, you are probably wrong. It is much more likely that you simply aren't coming across as someone who people feel they can tell these things to. You might read this and think, well, that's not (whichever person you know and might be thinking of), I know they can take care of themselves! They're a badass who throws bottles at cops (or whatever), they would definitely be able to say no! Well, not necessarily. Actually, a person can be very outspoken and still be unable to stick up for him or herself sexually. And in fact, survivors of violence are very often these very same tough-as-hell-seeming people.

Aside from the practical advice part of this, the how to make out with someone without unknowingly causing them to relive their histories of abuse or just ending up with them thinking you're gross when you never meant to be, I want to say a few things.

One is that no matter what you think about all this—whether or not you think you need this advice—consider the following: If you take my advice and you treat everyone in this way, you will be so popular! People will tell each other, "Oh, s/he was so sweet and great and..." Do you see where I'm going with this? Look, I'm trying to say you'll be better in bed, all right? You'll be the best date in town!

A second thing is that just because you're female doesn't mean you can't do things to people that might be triggering or putting pressure on them. Same goes for survivors of abuse. Being a victim does not make it impossible for you to victimize, and in fact we are statistically much more likely to pass on our fucked up shit. Being checked out during an encounter (as is common for survivors) is a really good way to not notice what's going on with your partner.

And, just because your partners are male doesn't mean you don't need to worry about these things either! Yes, more girls than guys are sexually victimized in this society, but given that pretty much every girl I know has some kind of fucked up story, that's not saying much. And the fact is, it can be harder for male victims to talk about these things, that there may be even less space where they can feel safe dealing with these issues, and even less consideration for their pain. So please, be careful with everyone, yeah?

The absolute, number one most important thing is to pay attention to the person you're with! Even if you're fucked up or really turned on or both. If you can't tell if they're into it or not, if they're being real quiet, STOP! Yes, it is *your job* to stop if you suspect your partner is not having fun. Maybe you don't want to make things weird but you know what? Things are already weird. You're making things worse.

The most sure sign you will ever get that something is definitely wrong is if the person who you're with seems to change suddenly, to become quiet or more withdrawn, tenses up, stops looking at you, or anything that makes you feel more alone suddenly. DO NOT assume they are alright! And then, don't hear just what you want to hear. If you stop and then you say "hey, you okay?" well, great, pat yourself on the back for being so rad if you need to, but then, if the person you're with kinda looks down or up or off to the side and says real quiet like, "no it's nothing, don't worry, I'll be fine," you know something? It is not enough to be like, "well, I tried, no one can say I didn't, so fuck it." I mean, do you like this person or not?! Sex is supposed to be fun! For both of you!

You can tell the difference between someone who's having fun and someone who isn't, I know you can.

The problem is that most people second-guess themselves, they think "well, I must be wrong, maybe she's shy about sex, maybe she's always quiet," or "it must be fine because he's a dude and guys always want to have sex, and because otherwise they'd say something, right?" Um, NO. Go with your gut, and if that doesn't work, err on the side of caution.

One of the first and most common causes of misunderstandings in a sexual context, and one of the most pervasive side effects of any kind of abuse history, is many survivors' inability to stick up for themselves in the ways that matter most. Abuse, especially if it happens when we were children or teens, teaches us that it doesn't matter what we want, it won't be respected, and if we don't say anything we don't have to face the fact that this is what's happening. If we say "no," and someone does what they want to our bodies anyway, we have to face the fact that a violation has occurred. However, if we don't say anything, we can later say to ourselves, "well, they didn't know, so they aren't so bad and I don't have to deal with the things I would have to if I admitted to myself what I know and feel, which is that they should have known, and that I secretly hate them."

The person you're making out with may literally be unable to advocate for themselves, to say to you, "Please stop. Please don't." They may be frozen by the fear that you will not like them anymore, or that you may think that they don't like you, or they may just be so far inside themselves that they cannot do anything. Because this is what happens: we freeze. Basically what happens to most of us when something is going on that reminds us of the bad things that have happened to us in the past is that we shut down, mentally and emotionally. We turn inward so that we do not have to experience the things that are happening to our bodies, because it is so painful emotionally and/or physically, and so terrible to have someone disregard you in this way. It's kind of hard to explain, but pretty much anyone who has been violated can tell you that's true. Your goal is not to be the cause of anyone doing this, ever, because it is a terrible, traumatizing feeling. If you do this to someone, it's fucked up, even if it was not on purpose. Good intentions are not enough to absolve harmful actions. You are responsible for what you do to others, even unknowingly. So pay attention!

Which brings up the other really big thing. If someone tells you something about their personal experiences with sexual trauma, however unlikely it may seem, you must believe them. Period. If someone says to you, "If you touch my elbow while I'm kissing you I will freak out," I don't care how silly it seems to you, just don't do it! And furthermore, try really hard to understand, to really understand that it's important. Maybe try to think of something outwardly weird or trivial seeming that freaks you out in some way.

And it won't always be as easy as that. Their needs might cost you something. Like this person you're hooking up with might say "I can't have intercourse, and also I can't go down on you," and you might think, "But that's the only way I can come." But you are going to have to figure something out because it's really not okay for you to try to talk them in to it, even by telling them how gentle and how great you'll be about it. Sorry, but you must respect them and their needs. It is a huge deal and very hard for a survivor to reach the point where they can even figure out what it is that they need, let alone tell you, so for god's sake, take it seriously when they can!

It's not easy to do these things. Mostly, it's really hard to learn how to be truly present in sexual situations. It doesn't come naturally to most of us, which is sad. But it is possible, and I think it's desirable to try to change the way we are in relation to sex. This is something our society just doesn't teach us how to do or encourage us to learn, and in a way we are all survivors of the fucked up things we're taught about sex. We learn that we're supposed to want it all the time, but also that it is shameful. We are bombarded with sexual imagery every day, yet we are told that we shouldn't talk about sex, especially not honestly; that sex is only okay to talk about if it's in alienating gross ways that aren't good for anyone's sexuality. And so lots of times we're so busy trying to prove something that we can't just relax and have fun. I think everyone can benefit from thinking about this stuff.

And while it doesn't come naturally, neither does relating to each other in these fucked up ways. We were able to learn that; we can unlearn it. It isn't something that happens all at once; it is a constant process, even for someone who thinks about this stuff all the time. But it can happen!

Other random things:

— It's great to ask people what's up and be willing to talk to them about it, but if they're not ready or up to talking about it, please respect that too. It doesn't help to be all macho about your new-role as a supportive partner and go around demanding that people open up and share with you, right now!

— Try not to take it personally if your partner says, "Yes, actually I am feeling freaked out and I don't want to do this right now." Don't give the person a guilt trip, or make it about yourself. They're having a hard time already and probably a lot of guilt issues too. You may have difficult feelings around this (hurt, shame, anger, confusion) but the person making the request is the wrong one to burden with those feelings. Be supportive in the moment, even if it's really difficult for you, and then talk it out later *with someone else.*

— One thing doesn't mean or imply another. If someone says they are okay with kissing, it doesn't mean they are fine with being felt up, etc. It means they are okay with kissing. It doesn't even mean that they will always be okay with kissing! All permissions self destruct at the end of an encounter (if not sooner) and you must start over each time unless explicitly told otherwise.

— Just use protection, even if pregnancy is not a risk. Your partner shouldn't have to ask, and they damn sure shouldn't have to argue about it. And if you can't get it together enough to carry any, then accept that you may not get to do certain things as a result. No arguing!

— And finally, this is a tricky one, and you can write me and tell me how fucked up I am… but listen—if you're under thirty and you're dating someone who is more than five years older than you, then consider the possibility that there may be a serious power imbalance in your relationship, which probably rules out any possibility of honest communication. You may think you're different, and you may really be, but everyone thinks their relationship is the 1% that is not fucked up, and 99% of them are wrong. I spent my whole teenage years dating people much older than me, and saying that it wasn't like that, but it wasn't until I had a partner of my own age for the first time when I was nineteen that I realized how different it was to be in a genuine relationship of equals where I felt like I could actually speak. Does my experience mean everyone is like this? No, of course not, but I've talked to plenty of other girls who know exactly what I'm talking about and have the same history. And an unequal dynamic means that the chances of someone enduring sex that they are not comfortable with or that may be damaging to them are increased many, many times over.

All right folks, that's it for now. There are people out there who want the opposite of every one of these things, who have drastically different experiences; but any rule of conduct that mostly comes back to finding out what people like instead of acting like you know is a pretty good bet. So go forth and be promiscuous with gentleness and affection and make the world a more tender place!

excerpts from letters

… I myself have never to my knowledge been abused sexually, but somehow it's turned out that most of the women I've ever seriously been involved with have. I do not pretend to know how it must feel or what it must do to you mentally or emotionally. I only really understand how it can make some people act and react to those close to them. How some things, some emotions are just shut down at times if not closed off all together, and how something as innocent as a kiss can, without warning, become a nightmare.

The first time I became aware that my girlfriend was abused, I had no idea how to react. I knew her father. Outwardly he seemed like a great guy. I liked him. He let me swim in his pool, and once at a barbeque he gave me a beer (I was only fifteen). He was aces. Anyway, after we had been seeing each other for a while, and things began to get more intimate, she told me about the things he had done to her in the past.

I was stunned. I didn't know how to react or what to feel. The only real emotion that I could hold on to was anger. I envisioned sneaking up on him late at night with a baseball bat and beating him stupid. I remember having a whole speech that I would recite while delivering the blows.

Of course, I didn't have the nerve to follow through. Instead I set his car on fire. He had a sporty little MR2 that he was very proud of. The ideal midlife-crisis-mobile. One night he had it parked on the street. I snuck out of my house with a can of gasoline, doused it, and watched it burn from three houses away. It looked cool, but ultimately it did nothing to help the situation. It didn't help her, it didn't help me, and he was heavily insured, so it hardly even bothered him. I realized that no matter how strongly I felt, it just really wasn't my business. Not in that way anyway. Nothing I could do would make it go away.

I never told her what I did. She didn't need revenge, she just wanted me to understand.

Since then I've been involved with several people that have gone through similar ordeals, and although I have never been able to completely empathize with what they went through, I have realized that just listening, and doing all that is possible to maintain a safe, non-judgmental, non-threatening and comfortable place where those things can be discussed openly whenever it might come up, is at least a good place to start.

—J

A WISH

...When he told me he'd been abused and didn't want to talk about it, I said OK, but we were best friends for five years and lovers for another five, and I never brought it up. I really regret that I didn't ask him about it when we got closer...

—S

...I don't really know how to write about this but... when my partner tells me about her abuse, or things related to it, she becomes really distant and closed off. She talks in a monotone, and it's scary. The stories are hard to hear, and I don't always know what to say or how to reach out to her. For a long time I just didn't know what to do. I would listen. I didn't think I had the right to ask her questions, and I didn't know how to comfort her. I didn't want to make her say more than she wanted to. I didn't want to make her talk about things she didn't want to talk about.

I realize now that on one hand, she really doesn't want to talk about it all, but on the other hand, she really, really does. She needs to feel like I really want to know, for my own sake, as well as to help her lessen the burden.

Often after talking about it, she'd be really angry with me. I've learned that even though she needs to talk about it in this distant and removed way, she also needs to let out the feelings, and if I just sit there and listen to her, the feelings of it all still remain bottled up inside.

I'm learning to trust myself more—to try and show her that I care instead of just acting scared. I ask her if I can hold her, ask what she's feeling. I tell her the monotone is scaring me. Sometimes, this is what she actually needs. She wasn't listened to or believed many times in her life, and sometimes just a few words will bring her back into this time and she'll see me and recognize that it's me and she'll let me hold her and let out the emotions that go with the story.

But sometimes it's not what she needs. She doesn't want to be held and she gets defensive if I ask what she's feeling. She says things like, "What do you think I'm feeling?" She yells.

This used to make me want to run away. It made me feel so worthless, and even now it is hard to understand, but I'm starting to see that this anger is part of her healing, part of her protections, and when it happens, I try not to get defensive. I might have to leave, but I try and do it gently—I tell her in a soft voice, a loving voice, that yelling is scaring me and that I have to leave for a little bit. I tell her where I'll be and when I'll be back. I don't do it in a threatening way—like I don't tell her to calm down. I just try to accept it all but also take care of myself.

I always make sure to bring up what happened and to try to learn what's going on, to show her that I love her and that she's safe, and that I'm willing to do the work, to love her and to know her and to care.

—*Anonymous*

Terrible What Happened,

...The first time I ever told the truth about the abuse I experienced, I put all these qualifiers first—saying it wasn't rape or anything, wasn't as bad as what had happened to other people. It was just being touched while I was asleep and watched while showering and things like that. The person I was telling it to said "Never compare it. Everyone I've ever met tried to invalidate what happened to them by saying it was worse for someone else. What happened to you was real. What happened to you was terrible. What happened to you counts. Don't belittle it."

This struck me so strongly. I had never believed that I deserved to feel as fucked up as I did about what had happened. That night I practiced writing in my diary, just writing what had happened without any qualifiers, just writing it over and over and finally letting it carry the weight and the pain that it actually held.

—*Anonymous*

Awkwardly, I Stumbled.

J.

When I was a boy of sixteen I fell in love. I fell for a girl who had a long story. She'd gotten hooked on dope young and wound up living through a lot of shit that many people do but no one should have to.

She loved me, but the scars from her past bulged tender. I'd been lucky. At that age, I didn't know the feel of sexual abuse. I didn't know what it felt like to sell the use of my body.

Awkwardly, I stumbled. I hated my body for reminding her of people who had violated hers. I hated myself because I was certain that every time she cried when we were together it was something I'd done. My narcissism and the self-conscious nature of my uncertainty in something new made me try to make it right. I wanted to fit it, fix her, erase the parts of the world that caused her pain.

I was lucky that she gave enough of a shit about me to teach me. She taught me that there were not words that could take away the past. Life is written in pen.

I learned to stop apologizing out of fear of her emotions. To just hold her because sometimes she needed to cry, because some people take note of anniversaries that are not happy.

We talked and talked. She told me about what it was like inside her head and I ceased to pity her but marvel at her instead. Life had hurt her but she had healed stronger. I was in awe of the courage that it took for her to laugh. The courage it took for her to trust. She taught me what it meant to be a survivor, to actively survive something not once but daily. She taught me more than I could ever put into words. I just want to thank her and every other teacher. Please keep teaching, you never know when you're teaching someone more than how to empathize, but something that will help them stay alive too.

Keep laughing, keep dancing, you don't always know how much your strength inspires. Many superheroes have torn capes, many angels have had scarred wings.

Embodied Consent

By Staci Haines[1]

The information that you receive from your body in the form of sensations, feelings, and intuition is key to the process of making choices. Survivors learn to override their feelings and acquiesce to other's wishes. I want to invite you back into your body now. From inside your own body, you can decide what you want sexually based on your own needs, desires, and values. I call this embodied consent...

The first step in embodied consent is noticing your own body sensations and signals. What are you feeling in your chest, your pelvis, your stomach? When you are doing something that you want to do, when your insides are saying "yes," how do you know this? For example, one survivor I worked with said her stomach relaxes and she gets a warm sensation there when she knows it is OK for her to go ahead. Another survivor reported that she felt an openness and warmth in her pelvis and a connection to her voice and throat when she felt a "yes." Check this out for yourself. How do you know when your body says "yes"?

Conversely, what signals and sensations appear in your body when you do not want to engage in a certain sexual experience? How do you know when it is not feeling right anymore? Another survivor reported: "I start to feel panicky in my chest and want to pull away physically. I usually try to talk myself into sexual contact telling myself, 'What's the big deal? Nothing bad is happening.' Then I don't listen to my body, I usually check out and have sex without being there." When you do not want to be sexual in some way, you may notice your breathing getting short, your stomach getting tight, or your body wanting to pull away. Pay attention. This is *you* communicating to you. What sensations in your body communicate a "no" to you?

---

1   Excerpt from Staci Haines, *The Survivors Guide to Sex: How to Have an Empowered Sex Life After Child Sexual Abuse* (Cleis Press: San Francisco, 1999), 106–108.

And what about maybe? Sometimes there are a number of seemingly contradictory feelings happening in your body at once. You may feel sexually turned on in your hips and vulva, and feel pulled away in your chest. You may feel a warmth in your solar plexus, indicating go-ahead, and be afraid and tight in your throat. What do you do then?

Actually experiencing contradictory feelings is familiar territory for most survivors. Consent then becomes a matter of distinguishing what sensations are what. One workshop participant noted, "I feel the consent to be sexual in my belly, it is a settled, sure sensation, and I can feel anxious in my chest at the same time. I am anxious when I am getting close to someone. I can count on this happening. It does not mean I do not want to be sexual." Another survivor shared, "I usually stop having sex when my stomach gets tight. I see now, though, that my stomach being tight is me feeling stressed about being turned on. It was so awful to get turned on during the sexual molestation that my body still tries not to do it. If I just relax and acknowledge my stomach and the fear there, I can go right on being sexual. My stomach being tight does not mean I do not want to have sex."

Sometimes we make choices about sex in our heads, because it seems like a good idea, seems to make sense, when we may be feeling something entirely different in our bodies...

You can end up feeling used, angry, or self-loathing after such a decision.

Consent does not always *feel* comfortable, easy, and joyous. Sometimes a consensual experience can bring up sadness, anger, or feelings of abandonment. It is important to learn the difference between experiencing feelings and wanting to stop what you are doing. You can do this by paying attention to your body and learning its language.

excerpts from letters

She had slept with a lot of people. It made me feel inadequate as a lover. I wish I'd been surer of myself. I think I made her feel like I judged her just like everyone else did, like I thought she was a slut when she was only trying to survive and figure things out.

I helped him write letters to his family and answered the phone so he wouldn't have to talk to them until he was ready.

Me and Allison have been together fifteen years. Every once and awhile we'll argue and it makes her really doomed, saying things like "This is always what happens! It's not worth it! Why don't you just leave?" We love each other so much, but it's hard to hold on to my self-confidence when she says things like this. I try to step back and not let myself get too wrapped up in those emotions and I try to look logically at it and realize that she's so hurt, and I try and explain why our relationship is different from other ones, and how we can make it through all this.

It feels weird to repeat myself over and over, but that's what she needs and so that's what I do. I feel sort of self-conscious, but I just tell her over and over that it wasn't her fault and that she's good. I mean it. She really is the most amazing person I've ever known.

When I start to apologize for being fucked up, that's when I need more comfort but can't figure out how to get it. If I'm apologizing a lot, then I know I need to get out of that relationship or situation.

Whenever he would get sad and overwhelmed by abuse memories, it would make me sad too, and then he'd have to be the one to get us both out of it by changing the subject or going out and doing something. He told me that it made him feel like he should never show his feelings, because he didn't want to make me feel bad. So now, even when I feel sad because of him feeling sad, I try to make an effort to not let it consume me. I try to focus on what he's feeling and needing. I can always feel the sad stuff some other time.

I hate it when people say "whenever you want to talk about it, I'll be there." I fucking never want to talk about it. I hate it, but I need to talk about it. I need them to want to hear. I need them to actually make an effort to bring it up, even if it's scary. I don't understand why they're not more curious. I would be. I would want to know. I swear to god, it's scarier for me than them.

Safe Sex for Survivors

Peregrine Somerville

Over the past couple of years I have read as many zines written by sexual abuse survivors as I knew existed. Not a single one made mention of the specific problems that we encounter when we are trying to be sexual, or included any practical information about how survivors might safely explore sexuality. For me, it was deep exploration of my own sexuality that first clued me in to the fact that I had experienced sexual trauma early in my life. After three years of celibacy and thirteen years of repressing traumatic memories, I became sexually active again. That's when the flimsy walls of my reality began to crumble. It was sex that finally released me from the illusion my mind had made in order to keep me safe. As I moved steadily through a haze of terror, re-entering a relationship with my own sexuality as the memory of my childhood sexual trauma resurfaced, it began to occur to me that sex might end up being at the very core of my healing process.

I've known survivors who are too afraid to even think about sex. I've known survivors who have sex indiscriminately, and without awareness. We hurt ourselves either way. Sexuality is central to the experience of being human. We *need* to be touched, it's just part of being a mammal. The kind of intimacy we are capable of having when we allow ourselves to be open and vulnerable in sex can be profoundly restorative, redemptive, and healing. It can reconnect us to our body, rouse emotion we never even knew we could touch, and ground us into present time—what can you think of that brings you more completely into the moment than an orgasm?

It's been my experience that making myself vulnerable, opening myself, and revealing the depth of my being to another person is vital to the process of recovery from sexual trauma. This is why I believe sex is one of the most effective ways to heal from abuse. You lay naked with someone, with yourself; sometimes you even enter another person's body, or take someone inside your own. It is one of the most powerful experiences a person can have, which is why it also possesses such devastating power to wound.

I want survivors to be able to touch this stuff. I don't want us to keep avoiding it, living in fear of it because of how badly we've all been hurt. Many of us still don't know how to do it, though. We can't rely on the culture that raised us to provide any healthy models of sexuality, that's for sure. And we'd better not wait around for them to address our experiences as survivors either. The best resource we have available is each other. We need to talk to one another, to our friends, our supporters, our counselors, our partners, about how to be safe with sex. We have to not succumb to our fear of sex.

Let's set some terms. First of all, I want to acknowledge that I'm not a highly credentialed expert on this. I'm not a sex therapist. All I have to back up what I write here is my own direct experience as a sexually active abuse survivor. When I say "survivor,"—and I will, over and over—I am talking about a person who has suffered some kind of sexual trauma at some point in their life. No matter what you remember or don't remember, whatever the perceived severity of what happened to you, you are invited to self-identify as a survivor. Mostly, this essay exists for you, but it also exists for your partner. When I use the word "partner" I'm not necessarily referring to a serious committed relationship. For our purposes, a "partner" is anyone you are having sexual contact with on a regular basis. Even if you're choosing to only have one-night-stands, this term still applies.

Okay, here we go

BOTTOM LINES

You don't always get to choose your limits. With my abuse material, I find that I rarely do. Limits tend to set themselves, and my task is to work with them, gently pressing up against them, expanding them whenever I can. We have to be honest with ourselves about what we want, what we can willingly do, and what we are unwilling to compromise. These are our bottom lines.

We set our bottom lines based on what we know we need, in sex and in a relationship, without exception. Naturally, so much of this depends on where you're at with your abuse recovery. Here are some examples of what bottom lines might potentially look like:

- I cannot get involved with someone who's into S&M because I know it's too triggering for me, and could be retraumatizing.

- I only want to sleep with my close friends; I can't be in a serious relationship right now.

- MY relationship with my partner must be monogamous, because it takes so much time and careful attention and trust for me to build sufficient safety in a relationship that to allow another person into this space feels like a desecration.

- I must have my relationship with my partner be non-monogamous because any kind of limits imposed on my life or sexuality by another person reminds me of the entrapment and control I felt during my abuse.

- I cannot be in a relationship with another survivor. I can barely hold my own shit together; I can't take on someone else's.

- MY partner must be a survivor too. I don't have the energy or the time to explain myself and explain what I go through to someone who doesn't share my experiences.

- I can't have sex with someone of the same gender as my abuser.

Your bottom lines might not be set up on a scale of polarities the way these ones are; they might not be as "hardline," but it's a good idea to use words like *must* and *cannot*. Your personal power within your own sexuality and your agency in your relationship with your partner will both strengthen immeasurably when you decide what you must have, what you can willingly do, and what you *will not* compromise. Keep in mind that many of these things will change. Some of my bottom lines are the exact opposite of what they were six months ago. Allow your needs to be malleable, but at the same time, understand and respect the fact that what you need right now is what you need *right now*.

TOUCH YOURSELF

Do not underestimate the far-reaching power of a positive relationship with masturbating. It is a way to explore our ability to have a positive relationship with our body, and it can be an amazingly strong way to give ourselves support with abuse recovery issues.

Masturbating brings our sexual focus back to ourselves rather than treating sex as a service to another person. No one else is there to tell us what they want; our desires are the only thing on the table. This in itself can be healing, and can help us to access our right to have needs.

Masturbation is also a way to explore our sexuality without having to contend with the sometimes complicated and confusing issues of consent that necessarily must arise when having sex with someone else. There's no one for us to have to communicate with except for ourselves, and the chances of anyone's boundaries getting inadvertently crossed are much lower.

For childhood sexual abuse survivors, our first exposure to sex was entirely on someone else's terms. It was coercive, and intended only to fulfill the needs of our abuser. Because we learned from the beginning that this is how sex is supposed to be, we tend to replicate these patterns now, in our adult sexual relationships. If we only sexually explore when we're with another person, we can be strongly influenced by their desires, or by our own desire to please our partner. We can confuse this with *our* desires, with what *we* want in sex.

When we shift the focus back to ourselves through masturbating, we retrain our bodies to be sexual for *our* pleasure and we give ourselves the opportunity to learn what that means. By fantasizing (aka solo role-play) and touching ourselves in different ways, and *then* moving into the realm of having sex with another person, we build a source of information and ideas to draw from about what we want and what's sexy.

Also—and this is really important—if you have rape fantasies or think about sexually abusing children and are turned on by this, it's a good idea to fantasize about these things while masturbating. These feelings need to get addressed. Masturbating is a great way to do this because everything you do is on your terms, one hundred percent. When these desires aren't acknowledged, are instead denied and shamed, they begin to become dangerous. If masturbating while fantasizing about being raped, raping someone, or sexually abusing children only makes you want it more, it is appropriate to take the next step in bringing it out into the open by seeking help from a counselor or other mental health professional.

Survivors need to develop a routine or ritual by which to get our sexual issues out on the table and work with this material. Masturbating is one of the best tools we have available to do this because it gives us the opportunity to heal with our bodies and our minds simultaneously.

SEX AND POWER

So you've decided to have sex with someone. Congratulations! Risks are good, and we have to take them! Now the trick is to figure out how to have sex in a way that isn't destructive or destabilizing to you or your partner.

The first decision to make is whether or not to tell your partner you're a survivor. You might not feel safe enough right away; you might not want them to know at all. Whatever you choose to say, however much you decide to reveal, you should be able to test the waters a little first by dropping a few hints.

For example, explain that you don't want to do certain things in sex because they are *triggering* or that you need to establish certain *boundaries* in the sex you have together. If they're keen on such survivor lingo as this, they'll hopefully ask more questions, and from there you can discern if you feel safe enough to talk more deeply about this stuff. If you don't feel safe enough to talk about it then you probably shouldn't have sex with this person.

You need to hold on to your power. Establishing your boundaries with a new partner either before you have sex or very early in the sexual phase of your relationship is essential to this. Otherwise you can fall into some pretty nasty sexual power dynamics and feel unable to talk about them.

One particularly hard power dynamic is that of simply not feeling able to have sex. There will likely be times when you don't want to have sex and your partner does, or maybe you want sex in your mind but your body won't allow it. This can be really frustrating for everyone but it's vital that you listen to these messages and accept them. If you attempt to override them, either due to pressure from your partner or from yourself, you can inflict some serious damage. We have to be more mindful with our sexual behavior than does a person who was not abused. If you are an abuse survivor your relationship to sex *cannot* be the same as that of someone who isn't a survivor.

And to the partners of survivors—as I have been one—I have this to say: If you want to have sex and your partner isn't feeling it, no matter how sudden this may seem, let it end there. Try not to feel rejected because this isn't about you. Don't go into your self-hatred. Don't sulk. Wasn't the whole point to feel the bliss of being deeply connected to this person? Ask yourself what would have happened if you had sex anyway. Is all the hurt and distance and potential retraumatization really worth it? This should be obvious.

TRIGGERS

A trigger response is when some kind of event or stimulus causes a person to respond in a way that either regresses them back to a time in which they were being abused or causes them to have an intense emotional response to the situation they're in or the person or people they're with. It's essentially the sudden arising of a survival state: *fight/flight* or *freeze*. When you're triggered, your partner can remind you of your abuser, may even physically resemble your abuser, and you may find yourself removed from present time, experiencing a flashback or body memory of the abuse. Your partner may touch you in a way that bears no apparent resemblance to your abuse history, and yet you feel frightened, anxious, angry, upset, nauseous, feverish, chilled, or simply uneasy.

If you're a survivor and you're sexually active, being triggered is inevitable. It's almost certainly going to happen. This is okay, because triggers aren't bad. They land us in a temporal state of emotional intensity, but they happen when it's time for us to confront an aspect of our abuse. A trigger is our body's way of letting us know what we need to be paying attention to and working on right now.

But triggers are still upsetting, so it's important that each of us devise a response system to being triggered so we can have a clearer idea of what to do when it happens. This is something we can do alone and with our partners. I would recommend doing both.

A good thing to do after you've calmed down from the initial flurry of being triggered, but with the experience still fresh in your mind and body, is to write a list of questions you ask yourself in order to figure out what you need when this happens.

For example:

- **AM** I dissociating right now? (more on this later)

- **DO** I need to sit up and look around the room?

- **DO** I need to come back into my body?

- **DO** I need to be with my partner?

- **DO** I need to be held?

- **DO** I need to be touched?

- **DO** I need to be alone?

- **DO** I need to put my clothes back on?

- **IS** there someone else I want to talk to right now?

- **DO** I need to just lay still?

- **DO** I need to get some water?

- **DO** I need to eat something?

- **DO** I need to get up and move around?

- **DO** I need to go on a walk?

- **DO** I need to meditate?

- **DO** I need a cigarette?

Laminate your list of questions with packing tape and keep it close to the place you have sex, under your pillow, in the drawer where you keep your sex toys and condoms, wherever you can get to it when you need it. Make sure your partner knows where it is. Give them a copy.

So you've been triggered. The first thing to do is to notice the feeling you're having and if you can, name it. "I feel afraid," "I feel dirty and gross," "My stomach hurts really bad," "I'm going to cry." You may feel an urge to ignore what's going on inside you and just keep having sex. *Fight this!* Say that you need to stop. Now your partner asks, "What do you need?" If they don't ask this, tell them anyway. You might not know exactly what you need. Look for that great list you made and try to find out by asking yourself those questions. If you're still not sure what you need or if you don't have a list, just try to be still and stay present with your feelings. This may be all that you need right now.

To the person supporting the triggered survivor: the focus needs to be on your partner in this situation. They need to be the one calling the shots because they're the one having the discomfort. As survivors are people who have had their power taken away over and over again, a supportive partner needs to *be supportive*. Don't try to fix or rescue them. They need to take that power back themselves, to make the situation better for themselves. Stay present with them. Hold the space intact.

DISSOCIATION

When a survivor dissociates they may not be having any intense feelings like would be found in an anxious or angry trigger response; they are simply gone, not in their body, not present in their experience. This response may be less alarming, it may even go unnoticed, but it is just as serious. Thankfully, there are still ways to return to present time.

It's difficult to dissociate when you're looking into someone's eyes. Eye contact can be awkward and scary and hard; it can also be incredibly intimate and can do a lot to keep you present in your body. The partner of a survivor may be more likely to notice their partner's dissociation than will the dissociating person. Ask them, "Are you here?" or "Where are you?" Be very gentle with this. Make it safe for them to come back.

However, eye contact can sometimes be too emotionally intense, and can even increase the dissociation. In such cases, it's better to simply sit up and look around the room. One definition of trauma is an inability to be in the here and now. The simplest way to return to the present is to connect to your external environment through the senses. Imagine that your eyes *want* to look around, and as much as you can, try to let go and simply allow them to take in whatever they want to perceive. Explore the perception of your other senses too: sounds, smells, physical sensations, etc. Supportive partners can ask a survivor who is dissociating to name three things they can see, and then three things they can hear, and then perhaps three things they can feel (as in physical sensations, which are different from emotions). This can break the dreamy spell of dissociation quite quickly.

What I've mentioned here are only the simplest of tools, a skeleton of a support system. The real substance of any functional method of healing is based on a dedication to caring for yourself and a strong bond with those you love. So take care of each other, and be patient. This stuff takes a long time. As a survivor, I know that my experience of myself, of my relationships, and of my sexuality is profoundly different from the experience of someone who was not sexually abused. This is okay. It's okay for us to have to work hard at what other people take for granted. The goal is not to return to some arbitrary center-point of normalcy from which we were taken as children. We are not deviants. The goal is to heal, to be on a continuum of healing. I am not asking for what I had before, I am asking only for redemption.

And special thanks to Laura for all the good ideas.

Listening

Cindy Crabb

Listening. It's supposed to be this universal thing we all know how to do, but in reality, there are a million different ways to listen. There is listening that is silent, like confession. There is listening where you quickly come up with your own opinions, or your own experiences and you add them in as soon as you get an opening.

Think about listening.

Pay attention to the different ways people you know listen. Figure out what it is that makes you open up to certain people and not others—what qualities of listening do they have? What responses do you need to feel heard?

Everyone is different, and what you need in a listener most likely won't be the exact same thing that the person you're trying to support will need. But *thinking* about listening instead of just feeling like it's something we should inherently know how to do is a first step.

Talking about sexual abuse may need a particular kind of listening. Below are some words about *active listening*, taken from a training manual for rape crisis counselors. (Active listening is also used in consensus decision making. It might seem strange and formulaic at first, but it's really a great skill and once you learn to think in this way, it'll stop sounding forced and will just become part of how you hear and process and listen.)

The purpose of active listening is to help you understand what is going on inside the other person; what their feelings are, what they are experiencing, etc. It's important because people are not always able to share what's going on inside of them. Sometimes the statements they make are coded or clouded. This means you have to decode or clear the message, and hear what they are really saying. The only way to know whether you are hearing correctly is to reflect back to the person what you are hearing from them. They will, in turn, let you know whether you are or are not correct.

The purpose is to show that you're interested, that you've not only heard, but that you understand (or are trying to understand) what was said. It helps to check your accuracy of decoding what they're saying. It gives them a chance to breath. It lets them know that you're actually there. It communicates acceptance. It fosters the person doing her own problem-definition and problem-solving and keeps the responsibility on her, not you.

When an abuse survivor says "I just can't tell anyone what happened," they may be saying any number of things:

— I want to forget it ever happened.

— I am afraid of what people will think of me.

— No one believed me before, why would it be different now?

— I am afraid of my feelings about it.

— I am afraid I will fall apart if I talk about it.

— I am afraid you'll think I could have prevented it.

— I promised never to tell.

— I don't know if I can really trust you.

... or a million other things

You need to find out the hidden feelings, otherwise you might assume the wrong ones. You can ask, "Do you mean...?" or "Are you saying...?" or "What does it feel like?"

Common errors to avoid while active listening:

— Exaggerating the feeling.

— Making it more intense than it is.

— Minimizing the feeling, not acknowledging it enough.

— Adding insight into the situation that is not there.

— Omitting or ignoring things that were said to you.

— Rushing to an insight that the person may be coming to—let them come to it themselves.

— Parroting what they said, rather than decoding it.

— Analyzing what has been said, why the person feels the way they do.

You should/should try to:

— Feel accepting.

— Want to help.

— Be able to take enough time.

— Trust that they can solve their own problems better than you can.

— Feel reasonably separate. You can empathize with her pain, but don't become overwhelmed yourself.

— Avoid evaluating the person, judging, or telling them what to do.

— Be aware of your own feelings.

What is Safety?

Staci Haines[1]

Most people think of safety as a "feeling" of being safe. While this is one way to judge safety, it is not always reliable. You can be in a very safe situation and feel unsafe because you are dealing with an aspect of your abuse. Or, because you are a trauma survivor, you may be in an unsafe situation and feel just fine. While feeling safe is important, it does not necessarily give you reliable ground on which to determine if you are safe, or safe enough to proceed.

What tells you that you are safe?

1. **HOW** do you feel in your body?

2. **IS** your physical environment safe and free of violence and abuse? (No one is hitting, kicking, punching or pushing you. No one is calling you names or threatening you or anyone you care about.)

3. **DOES** your partner, lover or friend consider your needs and wants and desires as important and as relevant as his or her own?

4. **CAN** your partner, lover or friend really meet your needs? Does he or she have the know-how, the tools, and the good intentions?

5. **DO** you have the power in this situation to act upon your own behalf? To take care of yourself fully?

6. **ARE** you making your own choices? Not being pressured, pushed or manipulated?

Asking yourself these questions gives you a way to assess whether or not you are safe—even when you do not necessarily feel safe.

---

1   From Staci Haines, *Survivors Guide to Sex*, 4, 35.

Write about the following, then have a conversation with a friend or therapist about what you wrote.

1. **TAKE** a sexual self-inventory. What have you experienced sexually up to now? What did you like? What did you not like? What do you know about your sexuality? What would you like to learn?

2. **TAKE** a piece of paper and make three columns titles "yes," "maybe" and "no." In the "yes" column, list all the sexual activities that you enjoy or think you would enjoy. In the maybe column, list all the sexual activities that you enjoy under certain circumstances or that you might be willing to try. In the "no" column, list all the sexual activities that you do not want to explore. Include both masturbation and partner sex. Now, look at your lists. Which column most closely resembles your current sex life?

3. **IMAGINE** an activity that is physically pleasurable to you, enlivening to your senses. It could be walking on warm sand, feeling the breeze against your face, touching your partner, having oral sex. Imagine yourself in that scene now. What kinds of sensations are you feeling which you experience this specific pleasure. Where in your body do you feel them? How much pleasure or desire can you take in?

4. **WHAT** sexual activity or fantasy would you like to try out? Be explicit. What's stopping you?

There are lots of folks who aren't familiar with the deliberate practice of getting consent. Learning the vocabulary of consent is like learning a foreign language. At first, you can spend a lot of time groping for words and awkwardly putting sentences together. These are the basics! Persistent practice will give you confidence to be creative, and you will eventually become fluent and able to express yourself in a way that feels less forced.

Discussions about consent echo similar ones folks were having at the beginning of the AIDS crisis—the initial resistance to using condoms gave way as it became clear that safer sex could keep people alive. Today, condoms, gloves, dental dams, and safer sex are a normal part of people's sexual lives and our shared dialogue about sex. Consent is a huge piece of healthy, affirming, and safe sexuality, and we want to see consent check-ins become as normal as rubber and latex in public discourse and private practice.

When it comes to the actual mechanics of talking about consent, there are no set answers. Writing this article, we were continually struck by the ongoing nature of the work. It's a process, and it can be a struggle. We're peeling back layers of silence and shame about sex—it can seem terrifying. We're inspired to keep moving because we're excited for a world without sexual assault, where all sex is consensual, and people communicate their boundaries honestly in all of their relationships.

Philly Stands Up! works with perpetrators of sexual assault. Our definition of assault is very broad—we roughly define assault as a situation where people's boundaries are violated, and there is a huge spectrum of actions that fit into our definition. Everyone needs to work on developing their consent vocabulary, but for perpetrators it is especially important, since a perpetrator has failed to get consent in the past.

It is appropriate and necessary in the aftermath of sexual assault for a perpetrator to go to Consent 101. We made up that term to describe the learning process we talked about at the beginning of the article. In Consent 101 you are exploring the fundamental ideas and language of consent and communication: the basics, the main ideas, how it feels to practice consent, and developing your consent vocabulary. This process can look really different in different circumstances, but we want to emphasize that, as a perpetrator, you cannot deal with sexual assault without improving your communication skills. If you can't communicate your boundaries, ask about someone else's boundaries, and act appropriately once you know a person's boundaries, you shouldn't be in romantic relationships. We also want to emphasize that good communication and consent do NOT only apply to folks you have romantic and sexual relationships with. Trust and boundaries are key elements of any sort of relationship, whether it's based on friendship, organizing, work, kinship, and/or romance. You have abundant opportunities to practice!

The most basic things to know and remember about consent are:

1) *You are never entitled.* You aren't entitled to sex or people's bodies or minds. You aren't entitled to sex because someone gave their consent last time, or it seems like they want it. It's your job to make sure that you and your partner's boundaries are on the table and respected, every time.

2) You *do* deserve positive, fulfilling sexual experiences. The shame and stigma around assault can be overwhelming. People are greater than any of their individual actions—you are not solely defined by it, but you are accountable for it. This can't be said without repeating: *You are never entitled.*

When you are tearing apart the negative patterns and poor communication that lead up to an assault, it can be overwhelming to imagine what getting consent actually entails. This is especially true in the heat of the moment, when you are face to face with a person you're interested in having romantic or sexual contact with. You should carefully and *specifically* think out your plan to talk about consent *before* you're in the sack with someone. If you do, you will be more likely to communicate clearly and less apt to cling to silence and shame. You should also make consent of all types a part of your relationships with all sorts of people—it's important to have consensual honest relationships across the board, and to be intentional as you create them.

We know that it's impossible to enter every situation knowing exactly what you want or what to expect—unpredictability is part of what's exciting about any kind of relationship. The more you can be intentional about what you want out of a relationship or encounter, however, the easier it will be to navigate it with integrity. We've heard lots of perpetrators say, in the aftermath of an assault, "I didn't mean for things to happen the way they did." It's likely that a lot of people, after they've made mistakes, certainly regret it and would do things differently if they could. Knowing what acting with intention feels like is a key piece of healthy relationships for everybody, and maybe especially people with a history of sexual assault.

Another piece of the consent puzzle specific to perpetrators is disclosure. If someone does not have all the relevant information, they cannot give informed consent. Negotiating sexual contact in the present *does* include an assault in your past. This is really difficult to talk about, and also completely necessary. Once again, if you don't feel like you can negotiate that conversation, you should rethink your decision to be in a given romantic or sexual encounter. It's pretty simple: *not* disclosing *before* hooking up means you aren't engaging in full consent.

We must take a moment here to offer the following disclaimer: disclosure must fit in with the needs of the survivor first. Sexual assault for a survivor equals a loss of control. A survivor loses the ability to determine what happens to their body and surroundings. A huge part of the process of healing is regaining that lost sense of control. A perpetrator's accountability process must serve that imperative—if you disclose details about the assault that the survivor doesn't want communicated, you are repeating the violation.

There are ways to talk about consent and sexual assault without naming names or breaking boundaries, and we'll offer some suggestions below.

It is up to you to figure out what kind of disclosure is within a survivor's boundaries. If you don't know, you could explicitly ask them (if that would be appropriate), or see if you can find out through your collective support networks. If you don't know and can't find out, err on the side of caution. You can talk about having a history of breaking boundaries and offer people the opportunity to ask more questions about what that looked like, without divulging sensitive details like names. Make sure you warn people in advance if you talk about details that might be triggering—you might be speaking to another survivor!

Talking about your history with perpetrating sexual assault is important for many reasons. Being accountable for your actions and to your community means owning your mistakes and working hard to restore trust. This trust goes beyond partners or potential dates. It exists among friends, housemates, comrades, and folks with whom you do organizing work and activism.

We are doing this work because it's worth it; because we believe that radical change is not just possible, but necessary. We do it because we are struggling with oppression and injustice every day and because change and possibility begins with ourselves, with our own relationships to each other. Because without genuine love, compassion and trust, we are all screwed.

Now on to the details! A great way to prepare to talk about consent is by role-playing. Having a few handy ways to open conversation is both empowering and an effective way to make sure consent conversations happen. We offer a few specific scenarios below. Practice these conversations alone; with a trusted friend; or even at a consent party, with a group of folks who want to become better communicators. Think about them, write them down, speak them out loud.

Disclosure is hard. Let's be up front about that. It's hard for a lot of reasons:

1. We may feel shame. Ashamed our actions; ashamed that we hurt someone; ashamed that we didn't know what we were doing; ashamed that we *did* know what we were doing.

2. Sex negativity is pervasive! Often, talking about an incident of sexual assault means we have to skate near or on top of the icy issue of S-E-X. Yikes! Even in cultures and communities where dishing about sex is accepted or encouraged, most of us have been exposed to negative messages about sex for most of our lives! This can make us feel disgraced, dirty, humiliated, and exposed—and not in the good way.

3. Fear of losing friends/dates. It is a very real possibility that once you talk to some folks about your past, they will feel nervous, angry, scared, or confused. Fear of losing friends or potential dates is a totally valid fear.

4. Killing the vibe. It might be hard to imagine interrupting a steamy moment with a new friend or date, one where the music is perfect, the sound of the passing trains is so charming, y'all are getting each other's humor, your hands naturally fall into just the right top/bottom position, it's awesome! How do you bust that vibe with something as heavy as your sexual assault past? Well, like we said earlier, folks used to (and lots still do...) say the same thing about condoms. But there are infinite ways to be creative and smooth while remaining honest and for real. And hey, what's a bigger turn-on than bangin' communication skills? No seriously, nothing.

One more thing: These conversations can go a million different ways. It's important to remember that you can't control the reaction and feelings of the person/people you are talking to. Focus on your own goals for this conversation. Your goals might include: staying honest; not omitting certain information; just getting through what you want to say; speaking calmly; etc. However, you should be ready for reactions. The person/people you tell might feel upset, mad, supportive, sad. They might not want to talk about it. Additionally, this might be much bigger than one conversation over tea. However this goes, it is important that you allow them to have that reaction. Take a deep breath and just be brave.

Ok, let's go through some potential scenarios of disclosure. The first is disclosing to a friend or people that you know well, in a non-romantic way. The next is talking to someone about your past right before you might cuddle/make-out/have sex/play/do it.

YOU KNOW THEM WELL

Why it's important:

1. So they hear it from you before they hear it somewhere else.

2. This is a crucial way to be accountable to your community.

3. You are doing the important, hard work of disclosure. You are deepening your trust. And hey, after you made the first move in your vulnerability, maybe they will feel brave enough to share something with you...

4. Your own healing. Keeping a big scary secret can eat away at you.

Here's a scenario... It's you and your pal/housemate.

It's a lazy Sunday morning. You are both awake, sipping tea while you cook a leisurely breakfast. The conversation moves into talking about dates and sex. Now might be the time. Starting the conversation might be the hardest part. Here are some ideas for how to start.

1. "I've been wanting to talk to you about something that's going on with me..."

2. "Listen, I want you to hear this from me..."

3. "I'm working hard to be accountable to my community, people I care about. I care about you. Part of that is talking openly and honestly about behavior I've asserted in the past."

POTENTIAL HOOK UP

Why it's important:

1. It is NOT consensual if they don't know all the information they might need to make an informed decision.

2. You are establishing trust.

3. You are setting the scene for all kinds of other important communication that should take place around sex (sharing pertinent health information, using barriers, checking in about boundaries, checking in about gender/body identity, etc.).

A potential date or hook up is upon you. Here's a scenario:

The two of you have been around the same scene for a while, but really hit it off at a puppet workshop. You were both flirting with each other via your puppets. It was totally hot and adorable. Now you're back at their house after drinking tea. There have been some deliberate hand squeezes, arm brushes, and lots of flirty talk. You kiss...

Here are some ways to start:

1. "I'm into you/ I want to do XYZ with you/ this feels good. But before we go any further, I want to check in about a couple things..."

2. "In the past I've crossed people's boundaries and I'm really committed to talking about that and making sure it never happens again..."

3. "I think consent is hot and important. I want you to know that I'm working on respecting people's boundaries and bodies and I have a history of struggling with that. I'm open to talking about that now or some other time, but I want you to know that."

4. "I want you to know that I wouldn't be here if I didn't trust myself to seek out and respect your boundaries..." (If you can't honestly and confidently say this, you should *not* be intimate with other people.)

If you can get through any of these scenarios, regardless of how they go, you should pat yourself on the back, give yourself a hug, and treat yourself to something sweet, because you just took a really big step and exercised a *lot* of bravery.

All of these scenarios are the possible start to some really hard work. But, if you are committed to change and radical revisioning of how we interact with one another, you've got to be committed to consent. The culture of consent is one that we are all responsible for shaping. Commitment to consent does not mean being the make-out police, being a stick in the mud, being overly sensitive, or any other hoo-ha type of myth that you may think of. The moment of an assault and the painful aftermath has a ripple effect through the community and reveals how interconnected we all are to each other. While we often see how harm to one or a few touches so many of us, the reverse is true as well. Positive, trusting, respectful, creative relationships and friendships are part of our survival. This tangible type of love is what moves us closer and closer to collective liberation. Our liberation, autonomy, and progress are bound up in each other. We need every member of our big beautiful community to flex those muscles of compassion, thoughtfulness, and integrity. Once you practice and learn yourself within the context of consent, you may be able to tap into creativity, confidence, and communication you never thought possible. And we don't know what's hotter than that!

Positive Consent for Dudes Who Get it On with Dudes

Nick Riotfag

I could feel his hard-on pushing through the front of his scraggly cut-off shorts, against my own swelling crotch. I was in a bit of a daze, electrified by his arousal, thirsting for the salty taste of his neck, intoxicated by the friction of our sweaty bodies throbbing against each other. Finally, the making out ebbed to a point when we each paused to breathe, smile, and make eye contact. I was hot, I was horny, I was ready for anything. Just ask, I'm yours, take anything you want from me.

With his arms around my shoulders, my ass in his lap, and our eyes locked, he opens his lips, pauses briefly in a smile, and murmurs in a gruff, soft, sexy voice:

"I'd really love to fuck you. But…. I want to get to know you first."

Huh?

Hold on. Back up. Maybe I should provide some context.

I'm a punk and an anarchist and I also identify as a queer guy. Well, more so as gay, but I sometimes sleep with non-male people. So maybe as "bi," but the gender "bi"nary is bullshit, and I feel much more identified with gay culture… or something. It's complicated. In any case, I've largely dated and slept with men, and I came out as queer and started participating in queer culture and activism before the punk/anarchist scene became my primary "home." In punk/anarchist scenes, I found the passionate political engagement, the unapologetic rejection of the mainstream, the fierce music, and the lifestyle that feels most compatible with my needs and desires. At the same time, even if I feel more at home at a squat or basement house show than a mainstream gay bar, it gets old having most of my anarchist male friends be totally straight, or "queer" in a way that doesn't involve dating men, least of all me. So I've always felt like I have one foot in each of these two very different scenes, and have never really been able to exist only in one without the other. This subcultural split has been the primary influence on the development of my sex life and how I experience and practice consent.

Some pretty significant differences exist between mainstream gay male sexual culture and that of punk/anarchist communities. As I think through my experiences, my desires, the norms and values I hold around sex, I can see how each community has shaped me differently. I recognize that each one has left me with certain things that I cherish, and certain things that I'm still struggling to overcome. Since I'm assuming, rightfully or not, that the readers of this book will probably have more context for punk/anarchist sexual culture than mainstream gay male sexual culture, I'm going to focus more on the latter, in hopes of showing some of the influences that have shaped me and some of the things that gay/bi male experiences can offer in learning about the complexities of consent. But first....

Some thoughts on punk/anarchist sexual culture, consent, and queer men.

In my opinion, the courageous kids who've pushed punk/anarchist scenes and communities to recognize sexual violence and transform norms around consent have begun to create a genuine shift in our shared culture. Over the past years of my involvement in this motley world of travelers and rabble-rousers, I've experienced significant qualitative differences in my sexual interactions with folks who've been socialized within these settings versus folks who haven't. Namely I've found the punk/anarchist folks who've found their way into my pants to be notably more open to verbal consent and adept at practicing it (and finding it hot rather than mood killing), less confined by gender stereotypes and narrow conceptions of what constitutes "sex," more comfortable with check-ins and communication about boundaries, and generally more compatible with my preferred style of getting it on.

Obviously, these are one person's experiences, and severe problems persist in every punk/anarchist community: continued belief in rape myths and survivor-blaming, "talking the talk" of feminism or consent while acting out the same shitty patterns, resistance to accountability or acknowledging abusive behavior, and innumerable other examples. Still, I've seen so many steps in the right direction: the presence of consent-themed workshops and discussions at most radical gatherings, the widespread circulation of zines and writing about consent and positive sexuality, emerging reading/study/discussion groups to focus on these issues in more depth, solid collective structures for community accountability in towns and at gatherings... These and many other signs point towards a shift in our whole way of thinking about sex and consent. In particular, absorbing and applying the feminist principle of politicizing the personal by insisting that these conversations be *public* and *community-wide*, rather than keeping them private as our own personal business, indicates that we as punks and anarchists are striving to radically change the way we collectively and individually do sex and consent.

So why hasn't this trend translated into lots of punk dudes loving each other with verbal consent as an established norm? There are a couple of factors that I think play into this. For one, although there are certainly all kinds of exceptions to this, in general I've observed that predominantly folks socialized as women are leading this subcultural shift toward consent and challenging rape culture. Definitely many anarcha-feminist men are following along and participating actively in the movement to transform sexuality in more consensual directions, but I've encountered far fewer punk men who speak consent fluently than punk women, both sexually and in all sorts of interactions. So for me, as a guy who primarily sleeps with other guys, I much more often find myself in bed with someone who may have attended a consent workshop, but not someone who's led one. Until the norms around who takes seriously and gets involved in pro-consent organizing shift so that men see it as every bit as much of a priority, then I think that one outcome is that consent will remain under-emphasized amongst men who sleep with other men. Of course, this definitely doesn't mean that men should be usurping the leadership of pro-consent organizing and education away from women (as has happened in so many organizations and struggles), but rather that men should recognize our responsibility and our stake in promoting and modeling consensual behavior in all areas of our lives, and participate equally in working towards that change on a community level.

Another unfortunate and frustrating dynamic that helps explain why punk/anarchist consent norms haven't rubbed off on queer guys more is that many consent discussions, workshops, and such still frame sexual consent in really hetero terms. I've seen consent talked about as part of a man's responsibility in protecting women, almost some kind of weird chivalry, rather than a mutual responsibility to be practiced reciprocally between partners of any gender. Even gender-neutral presentations are usually based on hetero experiences, and almost never refer to specifically same-sex situations. Now, don't get me wrong: I recognize that a majority of sexual violence is committed by people socialized as men, and directed against people socialized as women. As such, it's important to target straight men with the messages that will encourage them to act more consensually. Likewise, it makes sense that the people who are designing and communicating these messages, who in my experience are primarily women whose partners are straight men, would see a clear interest in encouraging their current and potential partners to think more about consent. But here's the problem: the exclusion of queer relationships and same-sex sexuality from consent models means that we dude-loving dudes aren't hearing really important messages that could transform our sexuality in positive ways. And this has a lot of negative consequences.

Even in my own life and sexual relationships, I have felt as if careful verbal consent was more necessary or important in sexual situations with women than with men. Why? I think it's partly internalized homophobia—the idea that queer sex and relationships aren't as important or as "real" as hetero ones, thus don't require the same care and consideration between partners—and also partly because we, as queer dudes, almost never have pro-consent messages directed at us from the punk/anarchist world. I have had sexual interactions with men that felt considerably less communicative or consensual than what their other female partners would lead me to believe they should be.

Likewise, I have seen kinds of harassment, objectification, and boundary-crossing directed from one man towards another be downplayed, laughed at, or even encouraged, when similar types of behavior directed by a man towards a woman would be immediately condemned. While punk/anarchist communities have made considerable progress in challenging patriarchal entitlement and promoting sexual consent, these interventions have primarily focused on the behavior of straight men in cross-sex interactions (as well they should). Unfortunately, this has meant that the experiences of dudes who get it on with dudes have largely been overlooked within these consent discourses—and as I'll talk about next—mainstream gay male messages about sex often don't promote a culture of consent, either. The lessons I learned about consent and sex from gay/bi male sexual culture were very different from those promoted in the consent zines, workshops, and discussions circulating within punk/anarchist communities.

What I've learned from gay/bi male sexual culture

From gay and bi men, I learned the crucial importance of safer sex practices. From as early as I came out, I had older mentors and peers who would talk with me openly about the pleasures and risks of sex, spaces and organizations where I could get condoms and lube, considerable awareness and education around HIV and STDs and their transmission, and a historical sense of how incomprehensibly crushing the losses of the AIDS epidemic proved to gay and bi individuals and communities. I also learned to accept with minimal judgment the diversity of tastes and preferences people experience around sex, from BDSM to fetishes to sex with strangers or multiple partners. I learned that we could talk openly about intergenerational desire and sex without denial and sensationalizing. I learned that sex for sex's sake can be found almost anywhere, in bars, on the street, in parks, online, and just about anywhere that men congregate. And I learned that no one can define my desires but myself, that together with my queer comrades we can reject everything the "experts" try to say about us, and that free, open expression of sexuality can be a part of a revolutionary struggle to transform society from the, ahem, bottom up (tee hee…).

At the same time, I learned of a sexual consumerism of the worst variety: a system mediated by internet sites and niche market pornography that reduced whole people to collections of characteristics, statistics, quantities. I learned that racist "preferences," body fascism, femme-phobia, and hierarchies of cock size were accepted as neutral, apolitical, and beyond critique because "we're just into what we're into, that's all." I learned to define myself in terms of my sexuality, with affirmations of my identity and self-worth derived from the number and type of sexual partners I acquired. In other words, I learned from gay male sexual culture some of the most hurtful aspects of conventional masculinity in terms of sex, on top of those same messages from dominant straight media and culture to which most male-socialized people have been subjected. This contradictory legacy I've inherited from the sexual culture of gay and bi men shapes my desires and how I experience them, and lays the groundwork for what constitutes consent for me.

Gay/bi Men and Verbal Consent

It's an uncomfortable but consistent part of my experience: amongst gay and bi men, I have not very often found partners who prefer verbal consent. On the one hand, something sounds frustratingly authoritarian in the declaration some anarchists I know have made that "any sex without verbal consent is assault," when the norms of one of the most central sexual subcultures in my life almost never condone or appreciate that style of interaction. At the same time, finding queer men who appreciate and practice the style of verbal consent and sexual communication that works best for me has been one of the most affirming, energizing, and relieving (not to mention *hot*) aspects of my sexual history. The rarity of it helps let me know when I do find someone who likes it the way I do that they're probably someone pretty special. But why do so few of the men-loving men—at least the ones I've known and been with—practice and appreciate verbal consent during sex? I can think of a few reasons.

One is that for many men who enjoy sex with men, that pleasure is fraught with guilt, secrecy, denial, and other painful emotions forced on them by the conditioning of a homophobic society. As such, many guys find it *incredibly* hard to speak the truth of their longings. Some find it repulsive to say out loud or to hear someone say the acts they do or long for. Particularly for closeted or straight-identified guys, verbalizing desire would mean talking on gayness in a way that they can't handle, so communicating with body language and acts, often through the filter of alcohol or drugs, provides the only means they have of living out their fantasies. Even men who are more comfortable with their same-sex desires and behavior have learned that their partners aren't always, and have found it more sexually promising (or even physically safer) to simply act and leave their unspeakable acts unspoken. Especially with sexual acts that are stigmatized more heavily for being "feminine," such as getting fucked anally, a verbal acknowledgment of one's desire can feel humiliating in a way that detracts from the pleasure of the act itself.

Another factor that diminishes the importance of verbal consent is the fact that a significant amount of gay sex is negotiated through online hookup sites or public cruising, both of which involve engaging only for a limited amount of time on an explicitly sexual basis. If I chat with someone on *Manhunt.net* or we make eyes in a park, we both know that if I head over to his apartment, it's for one reason only. As a result, many assume that consent has been pre-emptively communicated through someone's very presence. In many cases, especially online, the participants agree upon their desired roles or activities beforehand, leaving even less room for uncertainty. Of course, a world of nuance exists beyond the fact of mutual desire that complicates consent, but in a sexual culture that commonly involves brief, exclusively sexual, pre-arranged interactions, verbal negotiation in the moment is not always as central as in other sexual settings.

Still another reason why verbal consent isn't more prominent amongst men who have sex with men lies in the fact that gay male sexual culture involves some reflections of the dominant culture's sexual socialization around masculinity and desirability. "Real" men (who, of course, we who love men are supposed to desire above all others) are those who take charge, who know what they want and get it: active = masculine. Many gay men I know say that they long for a man who will be aggressive with them, take charge sexually and sweep them off their feet. There's something suspiciously feminine about asking first, about not claiming to effortlessly read your partner's mind and take charge to enact their desires; about being careful to listen to someone else's needs and boundaries. And nothing is less sexy, in a frequently misogynist and femme-phobic gay male culture, than that which is feminine. Since gay and bi men have our masculinity questioned, devalued, and denied by the dominant hetero culture around us all the time, many of us attempt to compensate by rejecting all things female or feminine. Sadly, this often manifests in hurtful, sexist ways, ranging from outright misogyny and disrespect toward/exclusion of women to chauvinistically rejecting any partner whose conventional masculinity isn't up to snuff. In reality, gay and bi men desire men with a wide range of gender characteristics—we femmes know that we can still get laid pretty often, too, in spite of their "straight-acting, masc only" bluffs! However, in terms of what's valued or socially acceptable, the norms of conventional masculinity dictate the standards, and one part of that involves pressure to be a sexual mind-reader and please one's partner without having to ask. Gay and bi men play both sides of that dynamic, both the butch top stud who aims to impress with action, not words, and the guy who's turned off by anyone who doesn't just take charge but stops to ask and check in.

Positive Consent for Hot Man-On-Man Action

So, in light of all these barriers to verbal consent, what does a hot man-to-man encounter with solid, positive consent look like? Well, it looks different for everyone, but for me at least, there are some key components. There are lots of zines and essays that lay out the most important basics: knowing your boundaries beforehand; asking at each new level of sexual activity; acknowledging nonverbal cues and body language as well as verbal cues; everyone should be sober enough to be clear on what's going on; and all that important stuff. What I want to add are just a few other things formulated with queer dudes specifically in mind. Pretty much all these are relevant to people of any gender and sexual orientation, but they come out of my specific experience as a guy getting in on with guys. So when I think about hooking up with a cutie, here's part of what I'm thinking:

Respect Yourself

Cheesy as it may sound, this is by far and away the most important part. Queers who love and respect ourselves are more likely to think about, decide on, and stand up for our boundaries; more likely to insist on safer sex; and more likely to be able to walk away from any encounter that seems sketchy, knowing that we will be able to find love, affirmation, and sexual release elsewhere. It is so hard to know what consent means, let alone give it and receive it, without first believing that we are *worth* being afforded the respect of consent. So please, take the time to learn to love yourself—you're worth it!

Negotiate Safer Sex First

Don't fuck around with your health. Before you start fretting over positions or roles, cover your bases around safer sex. Know your limits, communicate them clearly, and don't compromise—even if they're reeeeeeeally hot, even if they claim they can't get off with a condom, even if they won't let you blow them if you insist on a barrier, no matter what. Keep condoms with you or handy at all times when there's a possibility of having sex—don't rely on your partner(s) to have them. Get tested regularly, and if you have an ongoing partner, make sure that they do, too. Don't assume your partner(s) HIV or other STD/STI status, and don't assume that they'll tell you the full truth. Remember that acts that are safe for HIV aren't always safe for other painful or even incurable diseases (syphilis, herpes, etc.), and that even if you're already HIV positive, staying healthy means avoiding other infections. Make sure that you're consenting just to the sex, not to an infection or disease that could last a lifetime.

Ask What Style of Consent they Like

Truth is, some people just don't like verbal consent. It may be for some of the reasons I discussed above about gay/bi male sexual culture; it may be because they haven't challenged some of the crappy mainstream conditioning they've received from media, pop culture, and so forth; it may be for totally different and valid reasons that you don't have the context to understand. In any case, the important thing is for you to know what works for you—if you can't have a positive experience without clear, consistent verbal consent, then maybe you shouldn't hop into bed with someone who isn't willing to try it. SO ask up front, gauge how somebody prefers to communicate their desires, preferences, and boundaries—and be clear enough on your own to say "no thanks" if theirs don't line up with yours.

Fuck Out of the Closet

Here's a suggestion, which is sure to be controversial, but comes from my experience: it might not be worth the trouble to hook up with guys who aren't comfortable enough with their sexuality to be able to say what they want. Making it with straight guys may be hot, and it may give your ego a boost knowing you've bedded the unbeddable, but in my experience, in most cases it's not worth it. Save yourself the trouble and hook up with folks who are comfortable enough with themselves and their desires to be able to talk about them openly. It's not important what identity or label they use for themselves; what's important is that they're able to communicate directly about what they want, without having to be wasted to do it, or blundering their way through awkward sex silently. It's also safer—watch out for rough trade, aka dudes who'll let you suck them off but then work themselves into a homophobic rage at you after orgasm.

Negotiate Online

For better or worse, a lot of sex between men gets arranged on the Internet. Some think this is, in part, because the constraints of a homophobic society prevent us from meeting each other as openly as straight people can; whether or not that's the case, this is the reality we're dealing with and we can take advantage of it to promote consent. Talking through a computer screen can lessen the fear of rejection, desire to appear coy or indirect, and other things that make talking about consent harder. And however shitty the consumerism of online sex may be, the vast array of postings can serve as a reminder that if we don't feel comfortable with someone, there will be other options for sexual release. By posting our preference in an ad or profile, and chatting with someone beforehand specifically about the kind of sex we want to have, we can set up whatever norms of consent feel best for us. The risk of this, of course, is that pre-arranged agreements for what to do and how to do it with someone may lead them (or you) to believe that there is no need to check in verbally, to be aware of body language and nonverbal cues, to make space to pause or stop completely if something doesn't feel right. But if we choose to go the Internet route, we can use it as a lower-pressure way to set up consent practices beforehand that reflect our own needs and ideals.

Think about Consent and Gender

For me, good consent requires being aware of, and rejecting, gender roles in sexual settings. I know that I can't feel solid in the consensuality of a sexual interaction when everything—from who initiates to what acts we do together and who's penetrated by what—is determined by the gender role conditioning that strangles us, rather than by our own desires, needs, preferences, and boundaries. The impact of this socialization shows itself most clearly in cross-sex interactions, but pops up in same-sex adventures too. For instance, if a same-sex couple includes a more masculine or butch partner, gender conventions may dictate that that person shouldn't be penetrated, or should take the lead, or should act in a certain way based on gendered dynamics. This is understandable, in a mainstream heterosexual culture that conceives of sex so narrowly that it asks same-sex couples "who's the man?" or "who's the woman?"; it's hard to avoid absorbing the constant denial and ridicule of our right to sexual and gender self-determination. In any case, regardless of the gender of the partner who's hot for me, and regardless of whether or not I'm wearing a pink mini-skirt or overalls and boots (or both!), for sex to be fully consensual for me I need to be confident that everyone involved has some consciousness of how gender impacts our expectations about what we should do, and that we've all chosen to reject those imposed expectations in favor of focusing on our actual desires. (Of course, sometimes our desires may fall along starkly gendered lines, in ways that may feel uncomfortable to self-defined radicals who love to fuck with gender but can't seem to fuck without it. We can get stuck in guilt and reject ourselves for our illicit desires, just as Christian anti-sex bullshit wants us to, or we can stubbornly defend our most conventional longings without regards to the patriarchal and abusive patterns they may seem to uphold. Between this rock and hard place, the only way I've been able to find a place that feels good is just to talk with my partners as honestly as I can about my desires and how I feel about them and how they do or don't relate to my politics, and go from there. The point for me isn't to get our desires to conform to our political aspirations—desire will never submit to being civilized into such tidy ideological constructs. The point, as I see it, is to set out toward being as consensual and as critical and honest and as self-loving as possible. If there's any beauty we can find between our quaking bodies in this fucked up culture, it might be along those paths.)

Understanding the Role of Sex in Your Life In General

Positive, full, life-affirming consent for me also requires an awareness of the role that all sex in general, and individual sexual encounters specifically, play in my life. At different times, I have longed for, pursued, and engaged in various kinds of sex for a litany of different reasons: horniness, profound love and emotional connection, loneliness, curiosity, affectionate friendship, a sense of adventure and daring, boredom, indifference in the face of another's strong longing, a desire to please or to avoid hurt feelings, a need for resources controlled by someone else (rent money, a place to crash for the night, status or prestige), the pressure of masculine socialization to impress someone, to flaunt social norms, to sustain a lagging relationship, to piss off a third party, to avoid awkward silences... and those are just the reasons of which I'm consciously aware! Can I be confident that I (or my partner[s] for that matter) are choosing freely and eagerly to have sex if I'm/we're not conscious of the motivations behind our desires and choices? Of course, it's possible to get swallowed into feeling so anxious about our motivations that we over-analyze everything and never muster the courage for a kiss! Still, while avoiding that extreme, I've found that it's crucial for me to have ongoing dialogue with others, and most importantly myself, in non-sexual situations about how sex and sexuality fits into my present life. That way, when I'm struck with longing or presented with opportunity, I can make a decision based in a more holistic sense of myself, which more accurately reflects how I feel about a particular encounter. This of course relates to people of any gender and sexual orientation, but it stems in part from my recognizing the pressure on gay men to define ourselves as part of a community through sex. I've wanted to have sex at times to shore up my sense of gayness, to affirm the feeling of connection to community that I get though my identification as queer. But what I'm really longing for at those times isn't actually sex, but the warm feelings of inclusion and affirmation that come from being a part of a community. That realization shook me up a bit, and prompted me to ask myself difficult questions about whether or not sex I had based off those desires was truly consensual on a deeper level. The important thing, I think, is that now I have a whole new level on which I think about consent, one that considers the whole context of me and my life in my sexual decision making. Yeah, it's complicated, but it's important, and ultimately really positive for me.

Anyway, back to me and E. I smiled and exhaled, feeling more relief than I had realized, more than made sense in that hot and horny moment before having had the time to look back on it and appreciate just what that statement meant to me. I liked E because he was attracted to me, because he was a flirt and a slut and seductively charming. But whether or not I would have anticipated it, I liked it WAY way more when he affirmed that he wanted me to be more than just a body to get himself off on—he wanted to experience a connection with me that included but went beyond just our bodies. Let me be clear—this is not to pass judgment on anyone whose preferred type of sexuality is much more anonymous or less connected on non-physical levels. It's just an acknowledgment that my ideas of consent had to expand when I admitted that even with this gorgeous guy to whom I was quite attracted and with whom I would have gladly committed a litany of perversities, consent meant more than just getting horny and going with it. It meant for me in that moment a mutual recognition and affirmation of one another's humanity, one that truly created the space for me—or him—to say no or yes or let's wait or any number of other things. It meant listening to my body as well as my heart as well as my brain, and recognizing that I can't separate out those parts of me as if I'm not a whole, integrated person.

Back Safely

Anonymous

I'm in what I refer to as a hyper-consensual relationship. We talk about consent and try to practice consent when we're in bed, when we're not in bed, through letters, over the phone. It weaves throughout the fabric of our relationship. It is the forum for our processing, where we get to see how our relationship is growing, changing, become more and more intimate. We talk about language—what language empowers us, what language we feel comfortable with. I feel comfortable saying breasts, she doesn't. She feels comfortable saying vag, I don't. It's OK to have two sets of vocabulary, one for my body and one for hers. We talk about phrasing, about the connotations of things. We try to say, "Do you want me to" instead of "Can I." We *can* do a lot of things, and they might not be particularly uncomfortable, but do we *want* it? We struggle, with an imbalance of initiations—the conditioning we've received that makes it challenging sometimes to not only find and use our voices to express desires, but to even be in touch with those desires in the first place. The other night I asked her over the phone if she likes the way I touch her body when we kiss, because I'm not always sure. She said yes but that she needed me to check in more, ask for consent about specific touches before I do them. These were things I used to ask about, used to never assume. Part of me was so happy and relieved she told me, told me that these things I was doing needed to be worked on. But part of me wanted to cry and not touch her again, scared I had hurt her and couldn't take that back. Part of me hated myself. This is what we struggle with—negotiating, learning together, accepting that we are in a process and not perfect. Accepting that we are just trying, trying to be in a relationship in a way that hasn't been modeled for us, culturally. A relationship where we're moving beyond love and good intentions, moving into processing, communication, vulnerability, practic...

Everything escalated slowly and she would stop kissing me and look me in the eyes and say, "How are ya doing?" She would stop to check in with me even though I always said yes, and it made me feel like I was respected. It made me feel like I was safe. Because in the back of my mind, I knew that if, for some reason, I should stop feeling comfortable and if, for some reason, I didn't feel like I could speak up, she would ask again and there would be space to back out or slow things down. I didn't feel trapped, the way I had always felt before, like "I've gone this far, now there's no way to get out of it." She gave me a choice at each new level, and just because we had already done something before didn't mean she didn't ask for permission before doing it again.

Consent can be so fucking scary because you're opening yourself up to rejection. You're creating a safe space, a space where your partner can say no. But what's so hot, so empowering, so fucking amazing about consent is that the yeses really become yeses. The first time you hear no, it validates all the yeses. The first time you hear no, it's not really a rejection, a failure of any kind. It's a reassurance that when you hear yes, it's a yes, and they'll tell you when it's not. The yeses become erotic and the nos are signs of the safety and the trust that have been built, that consent actually works, that what you are doing is worth all the work, is right.

I assume everyone I come in contact with is a survivor. If they tell me otherwise at some point, then great, but I'd rather be conscious of my behavior than to hurt someone and find out after the fact that it could have been avoided with some simple consent practices. I've learned to ask people if I can give them hugs. I ask children if I can pick them up. I ask a crying friend if they want to be held, if

they feel comfortable if I hold their hand. I have a friend who is a massage therapist. "The first rule of massage is to always obtain consent first," he said. "But I realized," he continued, "that it's not just about massage. I have to apply the principles of consent to every interaction I have in my life..." I think about what he said when I sit next to strangers on the bus, when I help people at work, when I talk with friends. Consent isn't inherently sexual. It's about communication, about working towards creating safe spaces. I want intimate, private experiences to be safe, but I want to feel safe in public too. Thinking about consent in all of my interactions makes me feel like I'm making a start on some level, doing my part to make that happen. When we practice consent we create our own safe spaces, and then see where those spaces overlap with others'.

This was my introduction to an experiential understanding of the practice of consent, of what it really feels like and why it's so important: I remember sitting on the edge of the bed, making out, but making out really sweetly, with soft kisses, and I remember thinking to myself, "this is the best part." Then I remember jumping off the bed, pacing, my heart pounding, scared to death, with a pit in my stomach that felt like it was swallowing me alive. I felt like a little kid. I started muttering shit to myself and it just got worse and worse. I tried to force it, to go back and just keep going. I couldn't stay in my body, couldn't keep myself from being pulled into the vortex that left me curled up in a ball under the covers crying. I couldn't open my mouth and I couldn't look at her. I wanted to tell her that it wasn't her, that she didn't do anything, that it wasn't her fault, that I loved her—but couldn't say anything. She sat there for a minute and then I heard her say, "Do you want me to stay here with you or do you need space?" I couldn't answer so she made it a yes or no question and she asked again, "Do you want me to stay here with you?" I nodded my head yes underneath the protective layers of bedding. "Can I touch you?" she asked and I nodded yes again and felt her hand on my shoulder. "You're okay," she started saying softly, "everything's okay, you're safe... you're safe... you're safe..." She asked if she could hold me and I nodded yes, so she curled around me and held me softly and I started shaking and crying. She stopped asking me questions and just let me cry and held me. When I was done crying, I moved the blankets down off my face and I turned around and faced her. I wouldn't look into her eyes but she held my head softly until I did and she asked me where I was. "Are you here? It's safe now, everything's okay," she said. I had never dissociated and come back before. I had always had to sleep it off, wake up the next day groggy and confused. But we had talked before about triggers, about how sometimes I dissociated and what that meant for me, about what I needed when that happened. We had sat there together and read the *Support* zine, we went through the questionnaire about consent in the beginning of it. We had prepared for experiences like this. She practiced what we had talked about, and it was the first time anyone had ever been able to bring me back, and bring me back safely.

Different Needs

Anonymous

I was sexually abused when I was a young girl, and so was pretty much every girl I've ever dated. All of us have needed really different things. I used to be really "strong" and didn't like to talk about it at all. When people would push me to talk about it, it was actually just really bad for me. Now I like it when people ask me if it's OK before they touch me in certain ways, or when they check in when we're making out. My current girlfriend hates the word "OK." She doesn't mind asking *me*, but for her "is this OK?" makes her feel defensive. Like when your parents are worried about you and ask if you're OK when you're obviously not. "Are you OK?" makes her leave her body, but if I say "Do you want this," that works for her.

A past girlfriend really didn't want to be asked any questions. She just needed me to pay close attention and to be able to notice if she was fading out, and then to just stop and hold her.

A lot of the girls I've been with don't want to or can't be monogamous. This is hard for me because I really do like just being the only one and I have jealousy problems that I'm struggling with. Some of my stuff relates back to the abuse and how things were done to my body. My body wasn't loved or treasured or protected; and I just feel so bad about my body and about myself most of the time. I want someone to commit to only me, and to love me so much they don't want anyone else, but I also understand where they're coming from. I understand how monogamy can feel like someone owning and controlling your body, and I totally understand needing to not feel owned.

For a long time, I've struggled to be OK with non-monogamy, but I think from now on, I should probably talk about it before getting into a relationship. I should probably take it into consideration and maybe not go out with girls who don't want to be monogamous, because it always ends up just being such a painful and hard struggle when we already have so much to contend with. It's hard though, because when I like someone and am in that amazing, crushed out, beginning time, the last thing I want to do is talk about this kind of thing.

I think one of the other hardest things I've had to figure out how to deal with is when I think everything is going fine sexually, and then the person I'm with tells me that actually something was really wrong. Like she didn't actually want to have sex the last few times, or that she was faking orgasms, or that something I did was triggering. This is the worst feeling, and it is so hard not to just panic and be like—*"Why didn't you tell me?!"* I really did say that once, in this accusatory voice. It feels so terrible to have done this, I am trying to be really attentive and careful, and I know it happens because I can't be perfect and she is so used to pretending. That has been her defense mechanism for years, but it is still horrifying that I have added to the unwanted sex in her life.

When things like this happen, it is hard not to get scared and blame her for letting it happen. Really, I know that this is the worst thing I could do. I am trying to figure out how to feel just happy that she's finally telling me, that she's looking to me for comfort, and that she feels safe enough to tell me. Then when it's appropriate we can figure out ways to try and communicate better. But even if we figure out new ways, I know that sometimes they won't work and we just have to keep talking and caring and supporting each other.

Numbers

Anonymous

I have never been able to figure out a way to talk comfortably about consent. I think I am pretty good about asking other people, but figuring out a way to explain whether or not I want to be doing something is pretty impossible. I mean, if I want to be doing something, it's usually fine, but if I don't, or especially if I'm unsure, it's impossible. If someone asks "is this OK?" I always say "yes." Everything  is "OK," I mean, I can survive anything, right? So even the best of intentions don't usually work for me, and just the words like "do you like this?" are triggering. Even if they're not specifically triggering, they make me doubt myself, like "Oh, I thought I wanted this, but do I? What if I don't? Shit! How do I know for sure?!"

Generally when people ask me for consent, it not only ruins the mood I'm working so hard to maintain, but it also triggers me. Then I have to try and navigate whether or not I'm going to be able to get out of the trigger, stop thinking so much and get back to just feeling good. If they notice me flinching or withdrawing for a second and they stop and want to talk about it, then it's just over. Maybe I don't want it to be over; I just want to be able to work through it myself and forget.

I've never really known what to do. There are some things that have worked—like talking beforehand about what I need—like being held after sex. And asking them not to ask me things like "how was it for you?" There are just too many words and sentences that are triggering for me. But I love sex and want to be able to do it. I want to be able to ask for consent and give consent. If people don't even try, then that's frustrating too.

So talking beforehand and also trying to figure out ways to talk about what's happened during sex—but later, like when we are not in bed, and trying to figure out ways for them to not get freaked out if I admit to faking it or having a flashback or just not wanting to do something. It's important for me to be able to talk about it later, because I can't usually talk about it at the time, but that usually makes people feel like shit and feel guilty and then question every move they make, and they feel like they can't get anything right and I have to take all the initiative and give so much reassurance and that makes me never feel like doin' it, and that sucks too.

One of the things that happens a lot is that I am really sexual in the beginning of relationships, but when the relationship gets more serious or when it's been going on for a while, more things start to come up. My last partner came up with an idea. I have to say that the fact that he came up with an idea instead of me having to do it helped so much! He came up with a number system he would ask me 1–6 to see how I was feeling in a moment. We worked together to come up with what the numbers stood for.

1. **FEEL** like being held. No sex. Nothing. Not even sexual energy.

2. I want kissing but nothing past that. No moving against me in a sexual way.

3. I want to kiss and might be open to other stuff too.

4. I want to do stuff, but check back in a lot as we go.

5. I want to do stuff, and don't want much checking in, just check in before doing anything with the down-there parts and check in if you feel like I might be feeling weird.

6. **LET'S** do it!!!

Something about the number system took the weight off things. It made it easier and a little bit funny. I was totally able to say "2" whereas I would never say "I want to kiss right now but nothing else." Saying those words would have made me feel really guilty, whereas saying "2" just felt like a fact.

It didn't always work perfectly, but it was way easier for both of us.

Desiring Consent

Lee Hunter

For a couple years I co-facilitated workshops about consent and got to hear a lot of people talk about how they bring up consent and talk about sex. It is my hope to avoid wasting all the interactions I had over the years by conveying some of the wisdom that I learned from listening to people talk about consent. These conversations were really awesome and helped me learn to define consent and my boundaries. Thanks to everyone I have ever been in a workshop with! Talking about consent can be difficult at first, creating awkward situations. But as you continue talking about your desires, it becomes easier and easier, and for most becomes a prerequisite to any sex that occurs.

Consent is a term that people have to define for themselves, and people define consent in a number of different ways. Here are some examples from past workshops:

"Consent is never assumed." "Consent isn't defined the same way by everybody." "Consent is verbal." "Consent can be nonverbal including body language." "Consent is never assumed with strangers OR long term partners." "Consent is an ongoing process at each new stage." "Consent is only possible when healthy communication is possible." "Consent is knowing and respecting my personal and sexual boundaries and learning, knowing, and respecting the boundaries of my partner."

And another definition from the now defunct *Blackthorn* (Issue 3, 2004), a paper from Portland, OR:

> Consent is hard to define because there are so many different levels of communication (body language, flirting/innuendo, conversing, etc.). The only way to be certain that there is consent is through explicit verbal communication: "Can I touch you here?" "Yes/no you can/'t touch me there."

There is no set definition of consent. Developing your own definition of consent is an important part of the process of defining your desires and learning how to communicate them to others.

Healthy communication is a huge part of consent. Consent does not have to be a process that involves stopping and asking the person that you are with if they are okay all the time or if it is OK if you touch them on the breast or on the genitals—unless of course it needs to be that way. People communicate about sex in different ways, some are more verbal than others, while some find talking in the heat of the moment to be a real turn off. The important part is for you to figure out what method works best for you and the person or people you're with. Do you like it when someone asks before they kiss you or touch you in sexy ways? Or would you prefer to have a conversation and negotiate the kind of sex you would like to have prior to even getting to the sex?

Figuring out what you like and don't like is a huge part of defining your boundaries, and through the definitions of your boundaries it is possible to consent to different activities. Boundaries are applicable to all aspects of your life. They are the barriers we develop and articulate in order to understand why we say yes or no. Sometimes boundaries get pushed and occasionally they get crossed. When a boundary is crossed it can be a liberating experience or a violating one, depending on the situation. In many cases, the act of boundary crossing is the source of a lot of the sexual assault that occurs. In other cases, you learn that something you didn't think turned you on, in fact does. I cannot stress how important it is to know your boundaries. A good way to figure out what your boundaries are is talking with your friends and lovers about what you like, what's happened to you in the past, and what your future fantasies are.

Boundaries, like consent, are not fixed. Consent may be given at the beginning of a night and taken away by the end of the night. There is no set of rules about consent. There is no one definition of consent. Defining consent is a personal process, as you think about the situations you don't ever want to be in again and the kinds of places you want to go with your sex life. Unfortunately, many of the people reading this book have probably experienced some sort of sexual assault in their lives and that complicates things.

For those of you who are reading this who have not experienced sexual assault firsthand, I would like to leave you with a couple of things to think about. Many people have been assaulted—not just *women*. First I'd like to encourage people to talk about sex and abuse history prior to sleeping with each other. Sometimes people are not ready or don't want to talk about assault histories, so don't push a subject that a person doesn't want to talk about. This should be obvious. Second, people who have been abused usually, not always, have triggers. When these triggers are tripped, the person will checkout of reality and probably go somewhere else in their heads. Physically this can look many different ways: a sudden quiet when there had been a lot of noise; going still or corpse like; or staring off into space. Everyone's triggers look different and this is where prior conversation can really help. Sometimes there are certain actions that will cause the trigger to go off, like being grabbed from behind or feeling like you're getting smothered. You are more likely to be aware of when a person is being triggered if you've talked about it ahead of time. As far as I can tell, most humans are not mind readers and not always as observant as we'd like them to be, so talking about sexual history can really help.

My suggestion is to learn how to be verbal about your needs. As a person who has been sexually assaulted, it took me a long time to learn how to talk about my abuse history and learn how to have a sex-positive attitude, and now no one can take that back from me. I am not a victim. I have learned my strengths and how to fulfill my desires and I am pro-sex. And as far as I can tell, everyone has the ability to feel this way; it's not always easy, but it's possible! Sometimes therapy can really help, and I say this with the knowledge that therapy can take many different forms. I found that one of the most important things for me was finding other friends to talk about sex with and learning how to share my experiences with others. Learn your triggers—if you have them—and how to articulate them. It can really help in having healthier sex and helps to define boundaries.

Another issue that has come up a lot is consent and gender. While talking to many of my male friends, it has come to my attention that in the heterosexual world particularly, consent is thought to be a male-directed action. That men must always initiate sex and women say yes or no. I must admit that I am always in shock about this idea that women are not supposed to or don't initiate, but this assumption really does come up a lot. I'd like to just re-mind everyone that consent is not a gendered activity, in the het or queer scene. Consent is every individual's responsibility and communicating about sex is important no matter where you fall in the gender spectrum.

At this point, most of the discussions that I have about consensual sex are self-initiated. I have been practicing this kind of dialogue for long enough that I no longer find it embarrassing to talk about my sexual desires and boundaries with another person. Whether they are a one-night stand or a potential long-term lover, everyone gets the same speech. And it turns out that lots of people find it really hot to talk about what kind of sex they are going to be having before it happens. In most cases prior negotiations about sex have really worked out for me. This is not a fail-proof method, but my success rate has been startling.

Depending on the kind of sex you like to have, informed consent is absolutely necessary before any type of sexual activity is going to happen. If you are into kinky sex, then chances are you've already learned a lot about consent. Due to the kind of sex involved in BDSM, that scene has some of the best definitions of consent and practical ways of discussing sex that I have ever seen. When you are participating in activities that can be potentially physically harmful and cause hospitalization, it is absolutely necessary to have a negotiation and consent process. As long as sex is consensual, there is no limit to the things you can do and places you can explore.

Alcohol and drugs are not a great combination for consensual sex. There are many people who do not believe it is possible to have consensual sex if you have been drinking or doing drugs. This is an open question for me, since in my experience it has depended on the situation. However, it may be the case that an individual is not capable of making healthy decisions under the influence, and this needs to be taken into consideration when thinking about one's own boundaries and how to define them. It is unfortunate that sex creates so many uncomfortable and awkward situations for people, making it feel so necessary to pull out the goggles of intoxication. Our culture does not encourage us to communicate about our bodies and how we relate sexually to one another, much less about whether we are having healthy, fun, fulfilling sex with each other. It's a shame that so much pain comes from something that can be so damn fun.

Here is a situation in which consent worked out really well. One night I was out drinking by myself at a bar and I ran into a couple of friends. There was a person that I had not met before and I thought to myself, "Delicious, I'd like to make-out with that person." Several beers later, we were kissing in the parking lot out back. I invited him back to my house on the condition that we would not sleep with each other due to the fact we had just met and were both pretty drunk. He agreed and the next thing I knew we were in my bed, making out and groping. At a certain point it seemed like we would be breaking our verbal agreement, then he asked, "Do you think we should take this any farther?" I replied, "No, I don't think so. We agreed we weren't gonna fuck before you came here." He said, "Yeah, you are right." And that was the end of it. We kissed some more and fell asleep. I like this example because it reminds me that consent is totally attainable and I'd like to think it is possible for everyone. I also used this example because (let's just go ahead and admit it), the fact is that a lot of people get drunk and fuck each other. In many cases the sex that is had is not consensual.

To be clear for anyone who is hazy on this fact, having sex with people who are passed out is called rape! For some reason, I have heard a lot of people deliberate about this type of situation, which happens more than I can tolerate. If you have been assaulted, please talk to people that you trust and figure out a way to deal with the trauma—but survivor tactics are a topic for another essay.

Even though consent seems awkward and sometimes silly, it is a really great process that can enable lots of great sex. Healthy communication skills are necessary, as we learn to discuss the topic of sex with each other and become comfortable with the topic. Learning what your boundaries are and how to communicate them is one of the first steps to forming healthier sex relationships, regardless of whether you are negotiating with a one-night stand or a long-term partner. Boundaries can change over time, and consent can be revoked at any time. But most of all, I hope that you are all having lots and lots of really hot, steamy, consensual sex!

Supporting Someone Who's Reliving Sexual Assault

Janet Kent

What I want to talk about may seem overwhelming and scary but it happens sometimes and the more of us who know how to help, the better. Many people who have been sexually assaulted develop a condition called Post Traumatic Stress Disorder, PTSD for short. The National Institute of Mental Health defines PTSD as "an anxiety disorder that can develop after exposure to a terrifying event or ordeal in which grave physical harm occurred or was threatened." They cite personal assaults, natural or human-caused disasters, accidents, or military combat as experiences that can trigger PTSD. The disorder is characterized by various degrees of re-experiencing the trauma: recurrent memories, nightmares, frightening thoughts, and what I want to discuss here, flashback episodes. Other symptoms are sleep disturbance, emotional numbness, anxiety, irritability, depression, and outbursts of anger.

Though this cluster of symptoms has probably been around as long as people have been hurting each other, it was not diagnosed until men began to exhibit symptoms in great numbers during and following World War I. Before, women were considered by the medical establishment to be the only bearers of physical manifestations of a mental condition; the disorder was called hysteria and was generally considered a contrivance of attention-seeking females. World War I sent home men who had experienced more than their minds could bear. They relived their experiences of war, their bodies shut down; they could not function. Suddenly, doctors decided that this mental state, shell shock they called it, could happen to anyone, not only to members of what they considered the weaker sex. What had previously been viewed the folly of women became a legitimate disorder worthy of attention. Unfortunately, this attention usually consisted of institutionalization and heavy sedation.

However negative the treatment, at least people who suffered from this disorder had a name for it. They could see that the mind sometimes collapses under stress, that it is a normal response to unbearable strain, not a sign of weakness. As the women's movement of the 70s grew, women who began to examine sexual assault and its effects saw the symptoms of PTSD in many women who had been assaulted or had lived in abusive environments. People who wanted to create a supportive framework for dealing with sexual assault developed strategies for helping people who exhibited signs of what they called Rape Trauma Syndrome. These strategies were implemented and taught to volunteers throughout the network of Rape Crisis Centers and Domestic Violence Shelters and they still are today.

When I trained at a rape crisis center, we spent part of one short class talking about what to do if a client started to relive an assault. Many of the volunteers expressed concerns that they were not prepared to deal with such an extreme situation. Our advisor explained that it hardly ever happened and that she hadn't dealt with a flashback in all her years at the center.

At least we spent those few minutes on flashbacks, because within a few weeks, one of my clients showed up at the center fully in the throes of reliving a rape. She had been in an abusive marriage for years, during which time her husband had repeatedly raped her. Though she had been on her own for a while and lived in a different town from him, she still had nightmares and felt continually unsafe. I don't remember what triggered her flashback, but it happened while she was driving. Luckily, she was near the rape crisis center and was able to pull in there. She walked in shaking and staring straight ahead. I led her to the couch as she described her assault as it was happening. She was terrified.

First, I slowly put my arms around her and spoke in a low voice, telling her she was in a safe place. Here is the important part: since the person is not in the present moment, you need to get them someplace safe in their mind. This might sound silly but it works. As they told us to do in training, I told her to picture a safe place and to put herself there, a place where no one can get her and she feels free from any possible harm. I then asked her to describe the place for me. This gives the person something to do, a task to occupy the mind until the crisis is over. She told me about a boat. I asked a lot of questions about the boat and the area around the boat. No question is too detailed. The person needs to focus on this safe place. After a few minutes of describing her boat, she quit shaking, her heartbeat slowed down, and her eyes saw her immediate surroundings again. She was still upset, but the crisis was over. We talked until she felt okay to leave and I checked on her frequently for the next few days.

The fact is, you may never be around when someone you know relives a trauma. But if you are, remember these few things:

1. *Speak in soothing tones.*

2. *If you touch the person, be gentle as you comfort them, there's a fine line between feeling held and feeling held down.*

3. *Ask them to picture a safe place and to tell you all about it.*

4. *Ask a lot of questions so they really have to inhabit the safe place.*

5. *Once the immediate crisis is over, talk to the person about what happened, what triggered the flashback.*

6. *Make a plan to stay with your friend or find another person they trust to stay with them if you have to leave.*

7. *Offer to be available for the person to talk to or spend time with in the immediate future.*

8. *Remember, these symptoms may get better with time, but you may need to actively support this person for a long time. They are dealing with a lot and this flashback is just an extreme manifestation of what they may be thinking of every day.*

9. *While therapy is sometimes maligned in our community, it can be very helpful. When someone is dealing with this much mental stress, talking to a trained counselor is probably a good idea. Don't be afraid to suggest this option, and help them find a therapist.*

Some rape crisis centers offer free counseling to survivors, regardless of how much time has passed since the assault. They also may be able to give you some referrals to experienced counselors in the area.

10. *Keep up the support. Keep checking in.*

Self-Care and Crisis Management

Peregrine Somerville[1]

Lists

Write down everything you can think of that is beautiful, that makes you feel alive, or that you simply *like*. It's so easy to forget these things when we're in our lows—and, consequently, to forget why we even want to live—and reconnecting to them even by name can help bring them back into our lives. Here are a few of the things on my list: moments of total silence on a city street; freshly opened lilacs; the smell of old books; drinking water when I'm really thirsty; handwritten letters to loved ones, or from them; the color of my skin under a full moon; the wind; the color green, deep green; the feeling of velvet against my ears and cheeks; the smell of sheep; putting on clean socks. This is the comfort food of my life. When my mental health plummets it's my tendency to forget all of these things, but with this list in a visible spot, I can't forget them.

In addition to the list of things to live for, you can write a list of actions you know will help pull you out of your shit when you're in a bad way. Examples could be anything from taking a walk around your neighborhood to eating a good meal to spending time with your dog. Give copies of this list to your close friends and supporters so they have some idea of how to help you when you're not feeling okay. Also a good resource to give your support people is a list of warning signs that you're sinking into a bad place. The signs could be subtle indicators like circles around your eyes from lack of sleep, or more overt behaviors such as not leaving your bedroom for days on end. Even if these things seem obvious to you, it's important that you identify them to your supporters so they know to come to your aid quickly, when the warning signs first start to appear.

---

1   Excerpt from Peregrine Somerville, "Mental Health" in *Recipes For Disaster: An Anarchist Cookbook* (CrimethInc.: Olympia, 2004), 366–382.

There is one more list you cannot do without: a list of people you will contact when you're feeling triggered or panicked or otherwise distraught. Write this list when you're in a relatively level headspace because if you try to do it in an activated, highly charged mental state you may have a hard time remembering who you can turn to, which may prevent you from seeking support. *Always seek out support when you need it.* Keep the list somewhere accessible; laminate it with packing tape and stick it to your phone or your bathroom mirror, and make several copies in case you lose one. Even if it doesn't seem important now, it will be crucial later on.

Crisis

A panic attack can be one of the most distressing and terrifying experiences you'll ever have. You might not even know that you're having a panic attack; the accelerated heart rate, shortness of breath, fear and confusion may set on instantly and inexplicably, and you may feel paralyzed and disoriented, with no idea what's going on. Although coming down from an activating experience like this isn't easy, particularly when you're by yourself, it can definitely be done. Here is one highly effective approach that comes from somatic psychology, known as "Three Out, Three In."

1. **SIT** in an upright position on a comfortable surface like your favorite chair, or lean up against a something solid like a wall or a tree. Don't lie down, as this can intensify feelings of helplessness and overwhelm. If you're walking, try to slow your pace until you can get somewhere reasonably safe (meaning a place where you're not surrounded by other people, or in traffic). You want to be still rather than in motion so that your heart rate can begin to slow down. If at all possible, try to find someone you trust to come with you. If not, that's okay.

2. **ONCE** you've gotten physically still, allow your eyes to begin taking in your current surroundings. Try to let your gaze move around slowly, not looking for anything in particular but simply wandering, just noticing what's around you. Now say, out loud, three things you can see in your external environment. For example: "I see the clock on the wall. I see the green color

of the houseplant. I see the wind blowing in the trees outside." Whether or not you have someone with you, it's important that you say the three statements *out loud* because it draws your attention toward *speech*—an embodied action that affects heart rate and respiration—rather than mental activity, which may be spiraling out of control.

3. **NOW** allow your awareness to come inside. Don't close your eyes, as this can be disorienting and can lead to overwhelm, but do start to notice what you can *feel* right now. For example: "I feel the chair against my back. I feel a gentle breeze on my skin as it comes through the window. I feel a slight tension in my stomach." As much as possible, try not to assess or interpret what you're feeling. There's really no need to think about whether the feeling is pleasant or unpleasant, or what it "means" that you're feeling it, just name the experience and move on to the next thing you can perceive.

4. **REPEAT** steps 2 and 3 until you have completed the cycle (Three Out, Three In) *three times*. So by now you should have mentioned nine things you can see and nine things you can feel. There may be a longer pause each time you name something, a moment to take it in, and it's a good idea to go along with that because it helps your system slow down. If you're still feeling panicked at the end of these nine, begin another set and continue until the panic lessens. Remember, the objective here is not to float away on a cloud of peace and bliss, but to simply decrease the feelings of distress and overwhelm.

As you do this exercise you may begin to notice sensations like heat or shakiness in your body, or some deeper, more spontaneous breathing beginning to occur. This is a natural part of the process of coming down from the fight/flight response (sympathetic nervous system) and entering the orientation response (parasympathetic nervous system). As much as possible, try to allow this to happen without intervening too much. Your body has evolved to recover from life-threatening events by moving freely into and out of survival states of consciousness, like the fight/flight response. In other words, frightening as a panic attack may be, your nervous system knows how to come down from it, and the "Three Out, Three In" exercise can help this innate "deactivation" ability to come more fully online. It is one of the most effective practices for managing distress and panic, and you can use it anytime you like.

If You Are Not the One Falling Apart

As a support person, the most vital tool available to you is empathy. Supporting a suffering person is a challenging thing to do and it may feel stressful and frustrating at times, and yet your task is to remind yourself that your loved one is in pain. Try to bring yourself back to a time when you were struggling like this person is struggling now. Remember how it feels to need support, and how hard it can be to ask for it. Your role as a supporter requires patience, a clear sense of what you can and cannot offer, and a willingness to communicate this clearly to your loved one. It can get really hard and feel really scary. There will be times when you don't know what to do, or if there even is anything you can do to help this person you care for so much.

Do your support work as a team. Having a core group of dedicated support people will preserve your own mental health and help to avoid any one person burning out or becoming resentful. Meet together with the other supporters and check in with one another. Talk about how the process is going, what's working, and what needs to change. It really does help to be organized about this. Be honest with one another about your own needs around the support process, and take care of each other.

Some responsibilities of support people may include basic survival stuff like getting the person to eat, go outside, and get enough sleep. A person who is falling apart in a serious way may not have any self-care ability, at least initially. Part of the role of support people is to help the person reestablish a self-care routine, which can look like a lot of handholding at first. Make good use of the tools the person has available, like the list of ways to pull them out of their shit, when they are too bogged down by pain. You may need to take the initiative in getting your friend to see their therapist, or go to yoga class, or whatever other external resources they may be leaning on (besides you). If they are on medication, get them to take their medicine at regular times each day and if they run out you may need to make a doctor's appointment for them. Network with their family members—blood relatives as well as chosen family—who have seen them go through these types of situations, and find out what worked in the past.

It is not appropriate for you to try to "fix" the person, or to lessen their suffering because it's too painful for you to witness. It's said that in healing, no one can do it alone, but likewise no one can do it for you. As a support person it's your job to create a safe enough container for your friend to have their recovery experience, including all the pain that goes along with that. You cannot control their experience. You cannot make their suffering go away, and it will actually hurt them—and you—if you try.

The most important thing is that you stay out of judgment. You may feel for a time that you're carrying more weight or doing more work than you'd prefer, but you have to remind yourself of your love for this person, of everything they give you when they're well enough to give. This is someone you love. The role you play in their wellbeing is a gift you are giving, not a burden you feel obligated to shoulder. Stay open and be honest, with yourself and with the person you're supporting, about your own needs and limits. Yes, you are allowed to have boundaries, and in fact it is crucial, for you and for the person you're supporting, that you make them. Keep the lines of communication open, especially when you're feeling fed up or frustrated. Seek out support yourself when you need it. Most of all have empathy, always, no matter how hard it gets. Avail yourself to the person's suffering, and let it open you, and make you tender. In this way, the suffering of others makes us whole.

Things to do when you're having trouble staying present

Cibola

Blink hard. Blink again. Do it once more as hard as you can.

Make tea. Drink it.

Call a friend.

Eat a snack.

Jump up and down waving your arms.

Lie down on the floor; feel your body connecting with it. Keep your eyes open. How does it feel? Describe it out loud to yourself.

Make eye contact with your pet. Now hold it.

Clap your hands.

Breathe deeply. Keep breathing. Pay attention to your every breath.

Hold a stuffed animal, pillow, or your favorite blanket.

Alternately tense and relax some muscles.

Now "blink" with your whole body, not just your eyelids.

Move your eyes from object to object, stopping to focus on each one.

Wash your face.

Go outside for sunshine or fresh air.

Consent Workshop

The Down There Collective

Below are notes and discussion questions that we (the Down There Collective) used to facilitate workshops and discussions on communication and sex. We usually did a fifteen minute introduction where we gave people a sense of what types of things would be brought up and to lay out some guidelines for the discussion.

Next we did a puppet show to get people thinking about what communication around consent looks like; when communication is done well, when it's not, and when communication could be better. The puppet show is a humorous way to bring up elements of consent that can be difficult to talk about such as intoxication, gender, hookups vs. long-term relationships.

After the puppet show, we would lead a group discussion. We have listed some of the questions we used during the discussions. We didn't try to bring up everything listed, but used this list as a way of guiding our conversation. After a half hour group discussion, we would then break into small groups to have more in-depth discussions. In the small groups, we encouraged people to talk about and come up with practical steps for how they can improve communication and consent in their own lives.

Then we come back together to share ideas from the small groups and look at our growing definitions of consent.

We hope this outline can help you form your own workshops on communication and consent.

CONSENT–SEX AND COMMUNICATION

When people come in, ask them to write down their personal definition of consent. Tell them they can add to this definition during the workshop as new thoughts and ideas occur to them.

I. Intro to the collective and our goals for the workshop

Intro:

Introduce the group who's organized the workshop.

Discuss what led us to develop the workshop—both what sparked our interest and our own internal discussions around consent.

Share personal stories and goals; why we're interested in doing this workshop.

Overview of the workshop/agenda

Definition: consent

1. *To give assent, as to the proposal of another; agree.*

2. *Archaic: To be of the same mind or opinion. n.*

3. *Acceptance or approval of what is planned or done by another; acquiescence.*

4. *Agreement as to opinion or a course of action n.*

Goals:

- We want to redefine consent—to question and broaden our ideas. Define what consent means to each of us.

- What does consent mean to you?

- Being participatory and having upfront communication can apply to every area of our lives. We want to help create a society that's based on consent and not coercion.

- We want this workshop to focus on communicating, being upfront, and being positive. Equip you (and us) with examples of how to be more proactive in creating safe consensual spaces. (Will not focus on assault.)

- We want to discuss dynamics and factors that might influence how we give or receive consent such as age, power, relationships, etc.

- We want to look honestly at patterns in our own relationships.

- One of our goals of this workshop is improving your sex life! We think that consent can be hot and liberating.

- We want to create an open area for a healthy conversation in this workshop. We want to provoke thought and further discussion. There aren't many places where there are right or wrong answers. There will be a lot of open and unanswered questions.

Support Person Presents:

- This discussion could trigger difficult memories or feelings. We want to encourage everyone to be aware of your own emotional state. Just because this discussion is happening now does not mean that you need to deal with this stuff now.

- If you want to step out of the workshop for any reason, feel free. I am going to sit by the door and am here if anyone wants to talk to someone more privately during or after the workshop. I am going to check in with everyone who leaves, and it's fine to just walk by me, but you can also utilize me if you want.

Not Assuming / Agreements and Confidentiality

- We have a diversity of genders, bodies, sexualities and experiences in the room—we'll try to make this discussion as inclusive and participatory as possible and we'll try to use gender neutral pronouns for participants. Also, we use the word sex loosely in this discussion to encompass all sorts of getting it on (talking "dirty," smooching, making out, doing it, etc.).

- Most all of us have received conditioning thru this culture, ranging from body issues to imposed beauty standards to sexism and misogyny to heterosexism to religious/sexual morality, etc. So it can be really hard to speak openly about sex. Let's not judge each other's consensual sexual behaviors or interests in this space.

- Step up/ Step Back: If you usually speak a lot, step back to give space to others. If you usually don't speak much, step up and give it a try.

- Don't name names or identifiable info during this workshop.

- Please address what's said, not the person saying it.

We know this can be a difficult subject to approach openly and honestly, especially among strangers. So we're gonna open up to you and be a little silly and ridiculous and we hope you'll open up to us.

II. Puppet show

As you watch the puppet show please think about:

- The factors, dynamics, and issues at play as the characters give and receive consent.

- Positive and negative examples of consent.

- Think up questions you may have for each scene.

CONSENT PUPPET SHOW

Background Info

Puppets—we made them all human-like and non-gendered.

Music—between sets we played "Let's Talk about Sex" (but we mostly did this show around 2006!).

Scenes—we were behind a short screen and the puppets were in front of a back drop that could flip—party, bathroom, outside, living room.

SCENE 1: Clear Non-Consent

PJ, a clearly drunk puppet, and Seal, a sleazy sober puppet, are chatting and dancing at party.

PJ: I don't feel so good... I'm going to the bathroom. I'll be back.

PJ teeters into the bathroom. Seal follows.

SEAL: (concerned, yet smooth) Hey, how ya doin'? I just wanted to come in and check on you.

Seal reaches out and touches PJ's shoulder, arm, or side.

PJ: (Takes a swig of the bottle in hand) Yeah! Feelin' good, good time! (Swiveling) Whew! Don't worry about me... I'll come back to the party in a minute (sounding upbeat).

Seal steps toward PJ.

SEAL: Hey...I've been thinking about US. Missing US...

PJ: Well...

Seal moves in for a kiss. PJ pushes Seal aside, bends over the toilet and vomits.

PJ: I don't feel so clearheaded. I've had a lot to drink.

SEAL: Come on, this is a party—let's have some fun. Here, have a breath mint. (Goes in for a kiss again)

PJ: Hey, what the fuck? Give me a minute... (Sounding pissed)

SEAL: Just relax, don't be so uptight. You never used to be so uptight. Enjoy yourself.

PJ: Seal, I don't know about this, I don't feel so good.

Seal: Come on.

Seal pushes PJ backward and closes the shower curtain.

PJ: Hey wait. (distressed)

A moment later...

PJ: (muffled) Let's just go back to the party.

SEAL: Just another minute, baby.

A few minutes go by. Seal quickly leaves while the party goes on around PJ.

RAT CHORUS:

Rat puppet/s come up and sing to the tune of the "Oompa Loompa" song from Willy Wonka and the Chocolate Factory.

"Do you feel an inebriated person is capable of giving consent?"

"Do you make people feel un-fun or not liberated if they don't want to try certain things?"

SCENE 2: Clear Consent Scene

Puppet #1: You look hot tonight.

Puppet #2: You too, and I like your dance moves.

Puppet #1: Thanks, but I can hardly move with all these folks here!

Puppet #2: Do you want to go for a walk to get away from the crowd?

Puppet #1: Sure, I thought you'd never ask. Let's go to that park on the corner.

> *Two puppets say goodbye to other puppets, begin to walk. Party puppets disappear, music fades, trees appear and you hear murmuring between the two puppets ("It's so nice out here!" "What a beautiful night!" "That DJ rocked!" "Did you see what PJ was wearing?").*

Puppet #2: I'd really like to kiss you, is that OK?

Puppet #1: Yeah!

> *Puppets kiss, smooching sounds, enter rats.*

Puppet #1: Hey, do you wanna go over there where it looks more private?

Puppet #2: Yeah, good idea. It's cool that we're the only ones out here.

> *(More smooching sounds)*

Puppet #1: Mmm hmm. Do you mind if I take off your shirt?

Puppet #2: Sure. Can I take off yours?

Puppet #1: Yeah!

> *Trees move in, Shirts Fly Up.*

Puppet #2: "Ouch, can we shift over? I'm on a rock!"

> *(Smooching noises & murmuring)*

Puppet #1: Is that better?

Puppet #2: Mmmm, that feels really good. Do you wanna take off my pants?

Puppet #1: Yeah, thanks for asking. Can you take off mine?

Puppets go horizontal. Pants fly up.

Puppet #1: Can I go down on you?

Puppet #2: Na, I'm not into that but I'd like to keep going with this 'cause you feel real good.

Puppet #1: That's cool. I like this.

Puppet #2: What else do you like?

Puppet #1: Actually, I'd really like to touch you there too.

Puppet #2: Yeah, go for it! That's my favorite!

Puppet #1: Cool!

Puppet #2: Mmm mmm mm. Can you do it a little faster?

Turns to smooching sounds, murmuring, music fades on, trees cover puppets and all disappear. Back to the party scene again.

RAT CHORUS (singing)

"What are some non-verbal ways to obtain or give consent or non-consent?"

"How might you express that something happening is not OK?"

"Do you think consent can be erotic?"

SCENE 3: Sexually Transmitted Infections Disclosure Scene

Puppets making out, smoochie sounds...

Puppet 1: Hey, wait a second, there's something I want to talk to you about.

Puppet 2: Ok. What?

Puppet 1: Can we talk about STIs?

Puppet 2: Sure. I've been tested and I'm clean. Why? Is there something wrong with you?

Puppet 1: Ah... no, never mind.

(more smooching)

Rat Puppet: Cut! Take 2!! Let's try that one again!

Puppets making out, smooching sounds...

Puppet 1: Hey, wait a second, there's something I want to talk to you about.

Puppet 2: Ok. What?

Puppet 1: Well, before this goes any further I wanted to let you know that a year ago I had a breakout of genital warts from HPV. The warts are gone but I don't know if I still have the virus.

Puppet 2: Well, I'm glad you brought this up. I don't know that much about HPV so let's just smooch for now and learn more about it together later.

Puppet 1: Can we smooch *and* dry hump?

Puppet 2: Yeah! I love dry humping!

Puppet 1: Mmmm hmmmm!

RAT CHORUS (singing)

"Are you informed about STIs?"

"Do you get tested regularly?"

"How do you talk to partners about STIs?"

SCENE 4: MANIPULATED CONSENT

At the end of the party, as other puppets are leaving. Puppets are standing together (waving goodbye if they have arms that move). In the living room. PJ stumbles out.

B = Bigger puppet

L = Little Puppet

B: Bye, thanks for coming over

L: (To PJ, the drunk puppet from a previous scene) Get home safe! Drink lots of water! Call us tomorrow!

B: See you later

L: (To B) Wow, what a party! Our friends are crazy! Ha, ha. And you! You had some hot moves out there on the dance floor, babe!

B: Thanks sweetie, it sure was a wild party! Look at the house. Ahh— it's a mess, but I'm too tired to deal with it now.

L: Yeah, it's been a long night, but I've still got some energy left.

B: Really?! I'm exhausted!!! Let's clean up tomorrow.

L: You can't be *that* tired. I don't want to go to bed yet—c'mon, hang out with me.

B: (Sighs) Ok.

They "sit" down on the couch.

L: You were so hot tonight; I love it when you dance like that.

B: Yeah, that's why I am so worn out.

L: Here, let me massage your shoulders.

B: MMMmmmm, that feels good. It's getting me in the mood—to go to bed.

L: It makes ME want to (leans in to kiss) "smmmmmmmmooochchhh-hh." (Noise, not word)

B: (Scoots away, makes hesitant noise like) "Ehhh uhh."

L: What's wrong with you? Don't you want to kiss me?

B: Well, yeah sure. I'm just tired.

L: Oh babe, but it's not that late. Maybe we could just fool around for a minute.

B: Uhh, well... (Really hesitant, unsure)

L: (Interrupts) You know I'll make you feel good.

B: Yeah, I know, it's not that. It's just...

L: Baby, please, why do you have to make it so hard?

B: I'm not trying to be difficult, I really am just tired.

L: Fine, we can just go to sleep if you want. (Annoyed and sarcastic)

B: Don't be mad, I'm sorry.

L: You don't *need* to be sorry.

Moves in, makes kissy noises... They kiss and puppets rub for a few seconds.

L: Maybe we should go to bed for this... (Said is sexy voice, implying...)

B: Yeah, fine (resigned)

They walk off the set together, presumably to the bedroom.

RAT CHORUS (singing)

"Do you view consent differently for people of different ethnicities, genders, sexes, ages, or class?"

"Do you assume consent in a relationship?"

"How do you define consent?"

III. PUPPET SHOW DISCUSSION (15 minutes)

- What did you notice in the puppet show? First / Second / Third / Fourth Scene

- What are some of the unspoken issues at play?

- Positive or negative examples of consent?

- Think about how you perceived the characters? Did you assign them a specific gender? Races? What assumptions could you make about their past and/or the relationships the characters are in?

- What are clear ways they expressed consent or non-consent? What seemed to work?

- What problems did you see? What might be the root of some of the problems?

- What are some factors that can get in the way of real, honest consent?

You can also bring up questions that the RAT CHORUS asked. Such as:

Scene 1:

- Do you feel an inebriated person is capable of giving consent?

- Do you make people feel unfun or unliberated if they don't want to try certain things?

Scene 2:

- What are some non-verbal ways to obtain or give consent or non-consent?

- How might you express that something happening is not OK?

- Do you think consent can be erotic?

Scene 3:

- Are you informed about STIs (Sexually Transmitted Infections)?

- Do you get tested regularly?

- How do you talk to partners about STIs?

Scene 4:

- Do you view consent differently for people of different ethnicities, genders, sexes, ages, or class?

- Do you assume consent in a relationship?

- How do you define consent?

IV: Large Group Discussion (about 30 minutes)

What are some factors that play into the ways we give, receive, and understand consent? (The following issues below should be brought up. Otherwise ask about them directly)

1. Recognizing Boundaries—your own and others

- How do you give yourself or someone else space to figure out what you/they want?

Do you know what you want? How do figure this out for yourself?

How do you communicate what you want or don't want?

Have you ever been unsure? What did you do?

How do you give a partner space to communicate what they want?

- How do you know when someone else is consenting?

How do you know when someone wants to be kissed or to kiss you?

How are you sure they are fully present?

That they are excited to be doing what they are doing?

Do you account for cultural differences?

- How do people communicate their boundaries?

Have you interpreted passivity or silence as consent? What factors were at play?

Do you feel it's the other person's responsibility to say something if they aren't into what you're doing?

How often do you check in as things progress?

What signs do you look for? Verbal? Other signs?

When do you feel its OK to use non-verbal signs? When isn't it?

Are the signals you are sending clear? Do your words match your body language? (for ex. saying "no" while continuing movement); consistency in words and actions? How do you address it when someone else's words and body language don't match up? (for ex. saying "yes" but moving away or not responding)

How do you react when someone expresses non-consent?

- Consent in long-term relationships vs. hook up?

What assumptions do you make once someone's consented?

Have you made assumptions about consent with a long-term partner?

How do different types of relationships impact how and when we talk about consent (ahead of time / in the moment)?

- How can you communicate about safe sex and sexually transmitted infections (STIs)?

When might be a good time to bring this up?

What is safe sex to you?

How can you help partners feel comfortable talking about it / bringing it up with you?

Where can you get more info on safer sex and STIs?

How does how you feel about someone, your assumptions about them, or the type of relationship affect how you talk about STIs?

2. Power and Privilege

- What power dynamics might factor into communication and consent (privilege, gender, sexual preferences, size, race, age, class, organizational structure, sexual histories)?

How does age play into communication and sex?

How do you address different histories or unequal power dynamics?

How do you honor the experience of the person you're with when it has been different than yours?

How do you bring differences up and communicate about them?

How does racism factor into how we think about people's sexuality? History of racism and rape.

- How can we talk about histories of sexual assault?

How can we bring it up? When?

What about coming from a background where sexual assault is the norm?

- How does inebriation affect asking for or giving consent?

V. Small Groups: Practical Tools (15 minutes)

Introduce yourselves. Come up with ideas and practical examples to share with everyone else wherever possible

- Giving and recognizing consent or non-consent

What are ways to express that you are into doing something?

What are ways to express that you are not into doing something?

What signs (verbal and non-verbal) do you look for to know what another person wants to do?

What are signs (both verbal and non-verbal) that you look for to know someone is not into going any further or doing something in particular?

How and when can you bring up what you need to feel safe? How can you bring up your boundaries, history, and needs?

- How to talk about consent and communication with a partner

When do you bring up that you want to talk about what you are and are not comfortable with?

Is this different for a long-term partner vs. a casual hook up?

What are some ideas for improving communication around sex?

What can you do if you or your partner isn't sure what you want in the moment?

- Making consent hot

    Do you think communication about sex can be hot? Why or why not?

    How can we incorporate clear consent into "doin' it"?

    How can we make it fun and erotic?

- Communicating about safe sex and sexually transmitted infections (STIs)

    What is safe sex to you?

    How can you bring up your feelings about safe sex and STIs?

    When can you bring this up?

    How can you help partners feel comfortable talking about it / bringing it up with you?

    How does how you feel about someone, your assumptions about them, or the type of relationship affect how you talk about STIs?

- Supporting your friends

    What are some ideas for helping your friends talk about what they want and don't want and safer sex?

    How can you support your friends (and how can they support you) in being clear about what you want and don't want?

    Are there any situations (like a party or when there might be drinking) that you would want to make a plan with friends? What would the plan look like?

How does drinking or drugs play into consent and communicating boundaries?

VI. (Re)defining Consent and Closing (15 Minutes)

Definition of Consent

What are some key thoughts, phrases, and words for enthusiastic consent?

Did your definition change throughout the workshop?

Wrap Up

Hope we opened up questions for people.

This is an ongoing process in understanding our desires and boundaries and communicating this with others.

Encourage you to talk about this in your communities, to break down barriers to talking openly about this. Improving communication and understanding is both healthy for our relationships and can prevent problems.

excerpt of comic . . .

by Chris Somerville

I RECENTLY STARTED FOLLOWING YOUR ADVICE. THIS MORNING I MADE TOAST AND GOT OUT OF THE HOUSE AS FAST AS POSSIBLE

I WALKED AROUND MY NEIGHBORHOOD PICKING LILACS. I FELT SO MUCH BETTER THAN WHEN I WOKE UP.
IT WAS THE BEST WAY I COULD HAVE BEGUN MY DAY.

SOMETIMES I REALLY WONDER WHY I AM SO VERY FUCKED UP

MOM SAYS IT'S MY GENES

PROPAGANDA SAYS: FUCKED UP WORLD, FUCKED UP YOU!

BUT THIS IS WHAT I THINK: ME + MY KIND, WE COME INTO OUR BODIES AND FROM THE TIME OF BIRTH A RADIANT LIGHT EMANATES FROM WITHIN US.

AND WE MOVE THROUGH THE WORLD AND EVERY MOMENT IS AN ADVENTURE AND WE ARE SO BRIGHT, SO FREE, SO OPEN

BUT THEN SOMEONE CLOSE TO US SEES THAT LIGHT. THEY WATCH IT WELL UP INSIDE US EVERY DAY AND THEY WANT TO TOUCH IT. THEY WANT TO TAKE IT FOR THEMSELVES. THEY TRY TO SUCK IT OUT OF US.

THEY LEAVE BEHIND A GAPING HOLE. ALL THE HATRED, THE PAIN, THE SORROW THATS SURROUNDS US PULL INSIDE OF US THROUGH THIS HOLE, THIS WOUND. IT WIDENS AND DEEPENS...

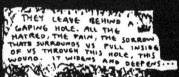

and so we learn to shut down

some of us never return

BUT DENYING THE EXISTANCE OF OUR WOUNDS IS NOT THE ANSWER

WE HAVE TO REMAIN OPEN ENOUGH TO SEE ALL THOSE THINGS THAT MOST PEOPLE CAN'T SEE

SOMEONE TOLD ME ONCE THAT THE VERY BEST THERAPY IS DOING THE THINGS YOU FEEL MOST PASSIONATE ABOUT AS MUCH AS YOU CAN

LITTLE THINGS THAT MEAN A LOT.

when I can finally **HEAR** myself again

I am holding the match

Bios

Thomas Herpich was born, along with his twin brother, in Connecticut in 1979. Tom now lives in Los Angeles where he has worked for the past six years as a writer and storyboard artist on the animated television show *Adventure Time*.

Cindy Crabb is an author of the influential, feminist, autobiographical zine *Doris*, which has been anthologized into two books; *The Encyclopedia of Doris: Stories, Essays and Interviews* and *Doris: An Anthology 1991–2001*. Her work has appeared in numerous books and magazines, including: *The Riot Grrrl Collection* (The Feminist Press at CUNY, 2014), *Stay Solid! A Radical Handbook for Youth* (AK Press, 2013), *Girl Zines: Making Media, Doing Feminism* (NYU Press, 2009) and *We Don't Need Another Wave: Dispatches from the Next Generation of Feminists* (Seal Press, 2006).

Andrea Golden is a popular educator, and coordinates the Language Justice, Cooperative Economies, and Popular Education Circles with the Center for Participatory Change. She is co-founder of the mobile home cooperative, Dulce Lomita, where she lives in the Emma Community of Asheville, NC with her partner and their three children, many beautiful and beloved neighbors, and seventeen chickens.

Consent Matters was Lee Hunter and Lauren Fontanarosa: Lee Hunter is a NYC-based artist. Lauren Fontanarosa lives in Portland with her partner and their two adopted dogs. She previously worked in sexual assault prevention where she developed and delivered training on consent for the group Consent Matters. She helped found the Hysteria Collective, a collective dedicated to raising awareness of sexual assault within punk and activists communities. After this work she went to school for a master's degree in public health and worked as a program coordinator advocating for LGBT elders for four years. Lauren continues to work in the field of aging services where she is part of a statewide team promoting coordination of and access to mental health services for older adults.

Shannon Parez-Darby is the Youth Services Program Director at the Northwest Network of Bisexual, Trans, Lesbian and Gay Survivors of Abuse. This group works to end violence and abuse by building loving and equitable relationships in our community and across the country.

Nick Riotfag is an anarchist, activist, crisis counselor and writer in the southeast US, who has written zines and articles on radical politics, intoxication and sobriety, consent, sexuality, and other topics.

Staci Haines is a teacher and lecturer in the field of somatics specializing in healing from trauma. She is the founder of Generation Five, whose mission is to end the sexual abuse of children, Her DVD, *Healing Sex* is available from www.healingsexthemovie.com.

Cleis Press is an imprint of Start Publishing, celebrating its thirty-fifth year of publishing books in the areas of sexuality, erotica, feminism, and LGBTQ fiction and nonfiction.

Philly Stands Up! is a small collective living and working in Philadelphia. We work with people who perpetrate sexual assault by leading them through processes that aim to hold them accountable for their actions and meaningfully change their behavior. Philly Stands Up! is community-focused and survivor-led. We embrace harm reduction, transformative justice, and anti-oppression frameworks as a means to strengthen and transform our communities and Movements into self-reliant, safe, and dynamic spaces. Philly Stands Up!

Peregrine Somerville is an activist, educator, and Somatic Experiencing Practitioner from the Pacific Northwest. He assists at professional trauma therapy trainings with the Somatic Experiencing Trauma Institute. His writing has appeared in *Entropy, Recipes For Disaster, Inside Front, Incendiary*, and in the lyrics of numerous punk and metal bands.

Anandi Wonder is a queer punk Californian femme who is now old, as will happen. She wrote this article so long ago that it seems like a message from a hazy, half-forgotten world, but upon reflection she realizes that her life has actually changed very little since then. She still lives in the same neighborhood, doesn't have a job, bikes around, looks like a dirty punk, hates cops and rich people and loves animals. There's significantly less dating happening though.

Courtney Chappell is an ex-artist and stay at home mom who lives in NC with her husband, daughter and tiny dog, Josephine.

Down There Health Collective was based in Washington, D.C. It existed actively from 2003 to about 2009, with occasional appearances to the present day. Down There worked internally to better understand our bodies and how to take care of ourselves and each other in a holistic way and externally to create safe and supportive environments to learn and share information, particularly around health, sexuality, consent, and gender by bringing up body and mental health issues that too often go unaddressed. Down There was known for showing how to do cervical self-exams, using puppets to talk about sex and healthy communication and sharing hands-on info on using herbs to support health.

Janet Kent is an herbalist, educator and writer who lives high in the mountains of Western North Carolina. She recently published *Ease Your Mind: Herbs for Mental Health*. You can read about her zine, her apothecary, Medicine County Herbs, and her residential apprenticeship program, the Terra Sylva School at medicinecountyherbs.com.

Kiyomi Fujikawa is a Seattle-based, trans-feminine mixed-race anti-violence organizer who spent a lot of time at shows passing out these writings when she organized with For Crying Out Loud. She currently works as the Queer Network Program Coordinator at API Chaya.

Jenna Peters-Golden has been a member of the Philly Stands Up! Collective since 2007 and is a founding member of AORTA Co-operative. She loves dreaming about the future but remains firmly committed to the present.

AK Press is small, in terms of staff and resources, but we also manage to be one of the world's most productive anarchist publishing houses. We publish close to twenty books every year, and distribute thousands of other titles published by like-minded independent presses and projects from around the globe. We're entirely worker-run and democratically managed. We operate without a corporate structure—no boss, no managers, no bullshit.

The Friends of AK program is a way you can directly contribute to the continued existence of AK Press, and ensure that we're able to keep publishing books like this one! Friends pay $25 a month directly into our publishing account ($30 for Canada, $35 for international), and receive a copy of every book AK Press publishes for the duration of their membership! Friends also receive a discount on anything they order from our website or buy at a table: 50% on AK titles, and 20% on everything else. We have a Friends of AK ebook program as well: $15 a month gets you an electronic copy of every book we publish for the duration of your membership. You can even sponsor a very discounted membership for someone in prison.

Email friendsofak@akpress.org for more info, or visit the Friends of AK Press website: https://www.akpress.org/friends.html

There are always great book projects in the works—so sign up now to become a Friend of AK Press, and let the presses roll!